MARY MAGDALENE

Adriana Valerio

MARY MAGDALENE

*Translated from the Italian
by Wendy Wheatley*

Europa
editions

Europa Editions
1 Penn Plaza, Suite 6282
New York, N.Y. 10019
www.europaeditions.com
info@europaeditions.com

*This book has been translated with generous support from the
Italian Ministry of Foreign Affairs and International Cooperation.*

*Questo libro è stato tradotto grazie a un contributo per la traduzione assegnato
dal Ministero degli Affari Esteri e della Cooperazione Internazionale italiano.*

Library of Congress Cataloging in Publication Data is available
ISBN 978-1-60945-705-1

Valerio, Adriana
Mary Magdalene

Book design by Emanuele Ragnisco
www.mekkanografici.com

Cover image: agefotostock / Alamy Stock Photo

Prepress by Grafica Punto Print – Rome

Printed in Italy

CONTENTS

MARY MAGDALENE

In one of his famous open sermons, the friar Bernardino of
Siena preached the following in 1427: "The Magdalene had
offended the Creator in seven things. First, of seeing,
pleasure. Second, in smelling, kissing, and speaking by her
mouth. Third, in try vanity of dress... than I commit,
looking lasciviously from her eyes. First, in adorning herself,
walking and mincing, by reason to make herself in the shame
legs, anotache... her charms. Fifth, in... her hands... too
... ... She has... effective cause for these
things, considering she was a vile person... love to her. First...
... ... Second... undulating... ... ...
I had released... and in death... ... ...
indeed, she was... vanity and... ... ...
... ...
more than all the vanity movement... ... ...
of Siena (sermon 46, translation from the Italian by Wendy
Wheaton)

These... ... ... reflect... the
image created by theologians in light around the figure of
the sinner Magdalene, and the way... ... ...
... should be transmitted and useful in a way that was...

INTRODUCTION
THE BEGINNINGS OF A MISUNDERSTANDING:
FROM REDEEMED PROSTITUTE TO JESUS'S MISTRESS

In one of his famous open sermons, the friar Bernardine of Siena preached the following in 1427: "The Magdalene had offended the Creator in seven things. First, in seeking pleasure. Second, in lustful kissing and speaking by her mouth. Third, in the vanity of dressing her hair. Fourth, in looking lasciviously from her eyes. Fifth, in taking pride in walking and managing her entire body. Sixth, in the shameless exercise of licentiousness. Seventh, in her resolution and attempt to sin. She had triple inductive cause for these things, causes that give a very strong drive to sin. First, physical beauty. Second, an abundance of material riches. Third, relaxed control and freedom to do as she pleased. Indeed, she was beautiful, wealthy and lived without being subjected to anyone. And this is dangerous for women, more than all the things aforementioned." (Saint Bernardine of Siena, Sermon 46, translation from the Italian by Wendy Wheatley)

These clear words incontrovertibly reflect both the image created by theological tradition around the figure of the sinner Magdalene, and the male conviction that women should be subjugated—not free in their choices, and certainly not in charge of their own body, which is seen as the object and subject of licentiousness and temptation. As the monk Honorius of Autun portrayed her in the early 12th century, she was "a common prostitute and of her own free will set up a brothel of sin and made it in truth a temple of demons, for seven devils entered into her and plagued her continually with foul desires." (Honorius of Autun, *De Sancta Maria Magdalena*)[1]

Compounding this image are paintings of the Magdalene such as the one by Correggio, who presents her as seductive and dangerous, or the one by Titian, who portrays her as a penitent prostitute with curvaceous shapes and voluptuous beauty, or the one by Francesco Furini, who shows her as sensual and indecent.

After the mother of Jesus, Mary Magdalene is definitely the female biblical figure most often represented in literature and art. She is not only portrayed in a carnal and transgressive key, but also and at the same time, in her redemptive aspect. Her meeting Jesus led to conversion, the mortification of her body, and a life of seclusion. For many people, she is the one who led a life of sexual excess that she later repented. To them, she is an emblem of humanity enslaved to sin and therefore a forceful reminder of another woman, Eve, sometimes considered the progenitrix of the world's evil. At the same time, however, the Magdalene is the prototype of the possibility of redemption. The image of the prostitute preserves the hope of salvation, so she can become the model of seductive eroticism who is pardoned to the extent that she transcends her own sensuality through a path of penitence and atonement.

Could there be a more powerful female archetype than that of the sinner who by contact with the Lord mended her ways, repudiated her body and tempting sexuality, and became a paradigm of mortification? Donatello's sculpture *Penitent Magdalene* (1453–1455) is emblematic in this regard.

Sermons, literature, iconography, music and today's movies continue to supply us overbearingly with the story of this woman marked by amorous passion and a sumptuous worldly life. She is presented to us much like a rich and elegant courtesan who renounces everything out of love for Christ, to whom she remains close throughout his entire life, all the way to the foot of the Cross.

A much more provocatory and complex argument has been postulated in recent years by a literary trend that presents the Magdalene as the partner or bride of Jesus, opening the thorny question of the Messiah's sexual life and the possibility of amorous involvement with his favorite disciple. See the director Martin Scorsese, who based his movie *The Last Temptation of Christ* (1988) on the homonymous 1951 novel by the Greek writer Nikos Kazantzakis. The film portrays Jesus as a man tormented on the Cross by the desire to experience a normal love story with the Magdalene, something he sees as a temptation to disavow for the good of humankind. Here too, while she is the object of nostalgic pleasure and the regret of not having experienced a life lived to the full, the woman is still seen as an enticement to resist in anticipation of a greater good: the salvation of humanity.

Much different is the outcome of the novel *The Da Vinci Code* (2003) by Dan Brown, where the author speculates that Mary Magdalene was Jesus's wife, a truth that the Church negated and hid in order to construct its power, exclude women and create a celibate, subjugated and easily manipulated clergy.

The questions I seek to explore in this book focus on the legitimacy of these more or less imaginative depictions. Just as there are no historical sources that testify to the Magdalene being Jesus's wife, the canonical gospels never say (despite the long, consolidated tradition to the contrary) that she was a sinner, a prostitute or a repentant for some other sin. What they do say is that she was a disciple and an apostle.

So how did this big misunderstanding come to be? It is a fallacious pretense that has weighed heavily on the collective consciousness regarding the female gender and on the role assigned to women in the Churches. It has for many centuries diminished the Magdalene's role as an apostle by transforming her into a reformed prostitute.

We will try to understand the birth of this error by entering into the folds of history, from the primitive Christian sources to their reception and interpretation, from literary documents to types of worship, and from artistic images to cinematographic portrayals. The scope of this research is not mere philological curiosity. The case of the Magdalene informs the very identity of Christianity because it poses crucial questions about the role of women in the Church, about the male monopoly over the theological and doctrinal patrimony, and about institutional bodies that have contributed historically to the marginal-ization of women. The revisiting of her memory is therefore an operation that we could describe as political, because it activates dynamics of change for the common good. This is usually called "Church reform".

Chapter 1
Who Was the Magdalene?

In the canonical gospels, female characters are often mentioned in a generic or anonymous manner, and not all of them are present or referred to in the same way. Mary Magdalene, however, is the only one to appear constantly in all the texts. This is a sign of her fame and authority within the group of the closest disciples who accompany Jesus from the very beginning of his mission.

Why the unusual name of Magdalene? In line with the patriarchal culture of the times, women were normally known for the man they belonged to, meaning they were his wife, daughter, mother or sister. But Mary Magdalene is not identified with a family role, thereby revealing the unusual position of a woman independent from her clan of provenance. Not being subjected to male authority enabled her to follow Jesus on his itinerant preaching, which tells us something extremely relevant about her personality, although we do not have sufficient elements to confirm or negate categorically whether she was a wife, a widow or a mother.

The mystery of her name

In the exegetical tradition that has taken hold over the

centuries, the name Magdalene is considered to derive from her birthplace, the village of Magdala, possibly located on the western bank of Lake Tiberias in Galilee, not far from the fishing village of Capernaum, the area from which also the other disciples attracted to Jesus's preaching hailed. Yet the name does not appear in evangelical scriptures. At the time of the narrated events, there was a commercial fishing center that carried the Greek name of Tarichaea ("salted fish"), but had this been her native town, she would have been known as "Mary from Tarichaea" or "the Tarichaean".

Thanks to excavations begun in 1971 under the archaeologists Virgilio Corbo and Stanislao Loffreda, and continued from 2006 to 2012 under Stefano De Luca (the director of Magdala Project), we have improved our knowledge of the position of the settlements around Lake Tiberias. Many of their names include the term *magdal* or *migdal* ("tower"). It has come to light that one fishing town was called Migdal Nuniya ("Tower of Fish"), of particular renown during the first century A.D. Another was named Magadan-Dalmanoutha, cited by the evangelists as a place visited by Jesus and his disciples (Mark 8:10 and Matthew 15:39). Several scholars including Joan E. Taylor (author of the paper *Missing Magdala and the Name of Mary 'Magdalene'*, 2014) deduce the latter to be Mary Magdalene's birthplace. Taylor explains how the epithet Magdalene seems to locate her place of origin, but the place of origin is extremely vague. There were many towers in Galilee, and no village was called just Magdala. It is therefore probable that Magdalene is a Galilean nickname that does not signify her place of birth, but rather indicates her position among the disciples closest to Jesus.

In addition, in Greek texts, the evangelists do not say "Maria from Magdala" but "the Magdalene Maria" (Mark 15:47, Mark 16:1 and 16:9, Matthew 27:56, Luke 24:10, John 19:25 and John 20:1) or "Mariam Magdalene" ("Mariam the Tower-ess"—Matthew 27:61 and 28:1) or "Mary called the Magdalene" (Luke 8:2), which may suggest that the name refers to a quality instead of a place.[2]

In her paper *Maria La Maddalena: ancora riflessioni su colei che fu chiamata "la Resa-grande"* (2003), the biblical scholar Maria Luisa Rigato proposes that we understand the name Magdalene not as a place name, but as a nickname, taking into account several patristic interpretations. Saint Jerome, for instance, traces the meaning of the Hebrew word *migdal* to "tower, fortress" (in the First Testament, the word is often an attribute of God—Psalm 18:3, Psalm 61:4, Proverbs 18:10, etcetera), thereby underlining her strength and greatness.

> "Mary Magdalene received the epithet 'fortified with towers' because of her earnestness and strength of faith, and was privileged to see the rising of Christ first even before the apostles." (Saint Jerome, *Letter 127* to Principia, Virgin of Christ. Eulogy of Marcella, Chapter 5)[3]

Origen of Alexandria also traced the etymology of the Magdalene's name, which he says comes from the Hebrew word *gadal* ("to become great"). He confirms that her name matches the meaning of the name of her hometown.

Indeed, the place name is interpreted as "greatness, growth". Mary Magdalene was great for the very reason that she followed Jesus and witnessed the mystery of his passion, says Origen (*Commentary on the Gospel of Matthew*, 1721-1722, translation from the Italian by Wendy Wheatley).

This motivated Maria Luisa Rigato to translate the Magdalene's name as "she who became great", an epithet that would indicate how in the communities of the origins, the relevance of this woman in her relationship to Jesus was already recognized.

Were this to be the meaning of her name, it would certainly be highly emblematic, because it would bring to the fore her role and importance within the circle of disciples. Whether "Magdalene" indicates a provenance (many scholars consider Magdala to be the Aramaic name for Tarichaea) or a nickname ("the Tower"), Mary Magdalene is along with Mary the mother of Jesus the best-known woman of the gospels, the most important disciple, cited first on the list of female names present in the collection of books by the evangelists, and remembered as the first witness of the Risen Christ.

Freed from seven demons

Although an unspecified number of women accompanied Jesus on the road through Galilee, few are mentioned by name. The synoptic gospels present Mary Magdalene as she who with "several women" including Joanna and Susanna followed Jesus on his itinerant preaching. As Luke the Evangelist writes in the *Parable of the Sower* (8:1-3),

> "Now it happened after this, Jesus made his way through towns and villages preaching and proclaiming the good news of the kingdom of God. With him went the Twelve, as well as certain women who had been cured of evil spirits and ailments: Mary surnamed the Magdalene, from whom seven demons had gone out, Joanna the wife of Herod's steward Chuza, Susanna and many others who provided for them out of their own resources."

The distinctive element of "Mary called the Magdalene" is being the woman "from whom seven demons had come out". The symbolic number seven indicates totality and fullness. It refers here to a particular kind of graveness, but it is not easy to understand what the demons represent. In coeval Hebrew culture and in the New Testament, demons are entities considered responsible for suffering, illness or mental derangement. They do not designate vices (such as dissolute living or moral deviation), but seeing that they are related to sickness and being possessed, they express distress and maladjustment, well represented for example in the episodes of demon-possessed individuals (Mark 5 and parallel passages). It is not the only time that the gospels mention Jesus freeing people from "evil spirits" as a sign of salvation thanks to the advent of a Kingdom of happiness announced to the poor and the suffering. Mary, we must suppose, was perhaps experiencing a difficult situation of malaise and alienation that might have derived from a mental disorder such as what today is called schizophrenia, or from another condition of dysfunction that isolated her.

Probably liberated from what the theologist Eugen Drewermann in his book *Die Botschaft der Frauen* (1992) calls "fragmentation of the self", the Magdalene finds in her meeting with Jesus the "therapeutist"(from the Greek *therapeutēs*), an "anchor in her existence". This turning-point in her life gives her a space of freedom that actually persuades her to leave familial security in order to follow the Teacher.

The gospels neither speak of the moral deviation that Gregory the Great later mentions, nor of "a life filled with all the sins" (Gregory the Great, Homily 33 in *Homilies on the Gospels*). There is nothing that refers to her being a prostitute. In addition, there exists no narration of her healing by Jesus, nor is it written who freed her. We must hypothesize that Mary was healed of a profound illness, of a grave condition of suffering and perhaps marginalization, and that her new state of liberation induced her to start following Jesus through new relational modes that entailed sharing and participating in the life of the group, as attested to by the word *diakoneo*, which means "to be a servant, to minister to" in the sense of carrying out an active role of responsibility.

The expression "providing for them out of their own resources" does not seem to refer to Mary Magdalene and her supposed economic wealth, but to the "many other women" who follow Jesus. Nevertheless, all of today's exegetical elements allow us to presume that Luke, in light of his community's economic situation, projects at the origins of the movement a model for the affluent women of his reference group, of whom he asks material support, indicating at the same time that whoever lives in an itinerant fashion needs help from others, in this case from women. In addition, the "service" that these female disciples offer must be interpreted not in a reductive way as a job of materially tending to others, but in a broader way as a missionary task. Drawn to the words of Jesus, they too detached from their families to place their material riches at the disposal of the group, sharing with the other disciples a new design of life and evangelization.

Jesus, the inclusive Teacher

The figure of Jesus reaches us through the selective filter of several of his followers, thanks to a delicate elaboration process of oral accounts and written sources. Several decades after the death of the Nazarene, the first communities were intent on defining their religious and social identity with complex dynamics of clarification and adaptation. Hereby, the place that women needed to occupy was an important consideration. Although the selection process of the sources obeyed the androcentric logic of the patriarchal societies, which were structured hierarchically and gave positions of responsibility only to men through stable and widely branched organizations inside the society, the evangelists could not avoid registering the freedom of relationships that Jesus succeeded in establishing with the women along his way. They recorded the active presence of the female group that shared with him their experiences, behaviors and yearning for salvation.

From the canonical gospels strongly emerges how Jesus succeeded in entering into an empathic dialogue with women, offering to listen, showing emotional involvement and scope for action. To women he addressed messages of hope, announced the requirements of the Kingdom of God, and asked them to make radical choices without ever considering them a separate or secondary category.

In contrast with a cultural and religious context that separated the sacerdotal class from the people, the worthy from the unworthy, the pure from the impure, the righteous from the sinners, kinsmen from foreigners, friends from enemies, and men from women, Jesus is described by the evangelists as a teacher who proposes meaningful relations based on the neighborliness of love (see the *Parable of the Good Samaritan*, Luke 10:25-37). This is the narrative reference frame in which women were inserted, freed from marginalization. Their body was no longer a reason for exclusion and discrimination. Indeed, Jesus allowed himself to be touched by a sinner (Luke 7:36 and following) and by a bleeding woman (Mark 5:25 and following) whose loss of blood made her impure. He touched the body, also judged impure, of a dead girl (Mark 5:41). The women's words were listened to and held to be convincing (*The Canaanite*, Matthew 15:21-28). Their prophetic gestures were defended and lauded (*Jesus Anointed at Bethany*, Matthew 26:10). They were no longer precluded from holiness (*Jesus Talks with a Samaritan Woman*, John 4). Their sins were forgiven (*The Adulteress*, John 8:1-11). There is not one word on the hierarchy of the sexes, not one on women's specificity. Although the gospels do not tell of a direct call on women as happens with the first apostles, it does not mean that women were excluded from the condition of being disciples, and this was an unusual circumstance in the Judaic environment at the time.

Discipless among disciples

Although a fair amount of limits hamper the sources at our disposal—sources that were born from theological and pastoral requisites—we must notice how all the canonical gospels transmit that Jesus was neither alone on his journey nor was he accompanied only by men. The group following him is composite, made up of women and men. However, the Greek term used in the gospels to indicate a disciple (*mathētēs*) is a translation of the Hebrew word *talmid*, which did not exist in the feminine, so we must hypothesize that every time the evangelists use it in a generic way, they may be including women implicitly. If we take into consideration the definition of the disciple as "someone who listens and learns from a teacher" we note that also the women present in the gospels belong perfectly to this designation, with the addition that several of them followed him from the very beginning of his public activity, adhered to his message and remained faithful to it, were present at the Crucifixion, witnessed his empty tomb, and announced his resurrection.

Some of the names mentioned in the canonical gospels together with "many other women" are Mary Magdalene; Mary the mother of James and Joseph, and the mother of Zebedee's sons (Matthew 27:56); Salome (Mark 15:40); Joanna the wife of Chuza; and Susanna (Luke 8:3). To these we must add Mary and Martha from Bethany, two sisters who, although they are not part of the itinerant group, occupy a place of relevance among those he "loved" (John 11:5). In an era that excluded women from studying law, Mary of Bethany, who "sat down at the Lord's feet and listened to him speaking" (Luke 10:39), is presented by Luke as a model disciple at the school of Teacher Jesus, capable of interiorizing his word, and giving the occupation of listening priority over the traditional and limiting family-related roles reserved for the female universe. Religious education, active or passive, was the prerogative of males only. In addition, she is the one indicated in the Gospel of John as accomplishing loving gestures—taking an expensive perfume, pouring it on Jesus's feet, and wiping them with her hair—that prophetically announce the entombment of the Messiah (John 12:1-3 and 7).

Parallel to her sister Mary, Martha is presented in the Gospel of Luke and the Gospel of John as a prototype of the disciple "serving" the community, meaning she actively carried out the task of *diakonia* (service) as an attendant for assistance and care. In the Gospel of John, Martha appears as the protagonist of a lively dialogue with the Nazarene that has deep theological content (John 11: 20-27). She is the one to pronounce the confession of Messianic faith: "Yes, Lord," she says, "I believe that you are the Christ, the Son of God, the one who was to come into this world" (John 11:27) and she is the first to show her faith in the resurrection of Jesus. It is relevant that John, in the name of the community, had Martha express this elevated theological concept. It is similar to the one Matthew attributes to Simon Peter: "You are the Christ, the Son of the living God" (Matthew 16:16). It is especially noteworthy if we consider that Matthew's verse constituted the foundation for the primacy of Peter, while John's verse did not lead to roles of authority for women within Catholic communities in the centuries that followed.

Nevertheless, the two sisters are represented as disciples of Jesus who establish with him a dialogue full of faith in hard work based on care and prophetic gestures. Evidently this reflects how the two types of service—that of the Word and that of *diakonia*—were practiced in several communities of the origins by women, too.

In addition to "several women", the Book of Luke says, "the Twelve were with him". Who were the Twelve and how did they interact with the female entourage? Theological tradition has taken them to be 12 men, appointed directly by Jesus in a privileged and exclusive relationship to continue his mission. In reality, the precise number of people following the Nazarene is not clear. There were men and women, and much uncertainty remains connected to the names and identities that emerge from evangelical sources. It is sure that the number 12 has great symbolical value in bible culture, because it indicates the recomposition of the original totality, in this specific case, the restoration of Israel, formed of 12 tribes. So the Twelve represent Israel, the new community reunited around the announcement of the Kingdom of God (Matthew 19:28), but just as the tribes—despite the fact that they carry only the male names of the descendants of the patriarch Jacob—implicitly included the women belonging to each people, the same can be said of the "new Israel". In other words, the number 12 refers to a symbolic and inclusive amount. Regarding this, I'd like to recommend reading *An Apostle without a Story* by Marinella Perroni, Part One of the book *Mary of Magdala: Revisiting the Sources* by Perroni and Cristina Simonelli, 2016 (English translation from 2019).

These interpretative hypotheses are increasingly expressed in the field of exegetics. Although problematic, they shine light on the limits of the traditional apologetic hermeneutic schemes, which projected upon the original evangelical tales subsequent theological criteria of a hierarchic and patriarchic type ("Jesus chose only males for his disciples and apostles, giving them tasks of responsibility"). In addition, said hypotheses give visibility to the female figures and the roles they played in the first communities.

The "hermeneutics of suspicion" (as defined by Elisabeth Schüssler Fiorenza in her book *In Memory of Her: A Feminist Theological Reconstruction of Christian Origins*, 1983) and the "exegesis *ex silentio*" (as defined by Carla Ricci in her book *Maria di Magdala e le molte altre*, 1991) encourage us to look for the presence of women beyond the voids and instances of oblivion in the sources, despite the androcentric contexts of ancient cultures that considered the female presence implicit or unimportant, as emerges in the gospels when they say, "Now four thousand men had eaten, to say nothing of women and children" (Matthew 15:38). Women were entitled to only a marginal role.

All this notwithstanding, women did not completely disappear from the texts of the first centuries. To the contrary, where they emerge they appear as significant figures in a vast range of situations. They listen, they ask questions, they attend to the comfort of others, they love, share, give testimony, upset people and transgress. They have roles as disciples, apostles, deacons, prophetesses, missionaries, collaborators and more (Romans 16:1 and following). Despite efforts aimed at diminishing its worth, the female presence could not be erased evidently due to its social and religious relevance. Among Jesus's Galilean disciples, Mary the Magdalene certainly holds a highly significant place.

At the foot of the Cross

"There were some women watching from a distance. Among them were Mary of Magdala, Mary who was the mother of James the younger and Josef, and Salome. These used to follow him and look after him while he was in Galilee. And many other women were there who had come up to Jerusalem with him." (Mark 15:40-41).

In the gospels' narration, the female disciples who

accompany Jesus since the beginning of his activity in Galilee (these belong to a much bigger group than the three women named here) do not only represent the "real followers"—those who abandoned their security to place themselves at the service of the Kingdom—but they also function as guarantors of the triple testimony that is the fundament of the formula of faith of the primitive communities: Christ died, was buried, and rose again (Acts 2:23-24 and I Corinthians 15:3-4). They are the ones who witness the crucifixion of Jesus (Mark 15:40-41; Matthew 27:55-56; Luke 23:49; John 19:25), his burial (Mark 15:47; Matthew 27:61; Luke 23:55-56), and at the empty tomb, they were the first to hear and announce the resurrection (Mark 16:1-8; Matthew 28:1-10; Luke 24:1-11; John 20:1-18).

In all four accounts of the Passion, albeit with the peculiarity of single narrative elements due to the diverse sensibility and requirements of the evangelists, the Magdalene is the only one to be always named, confirming her role as the custodian and guarantor of foundational experiences for the disciples' faith in the resurrection of Christ. Indeed, from faith in the Risen One were born preaching, missionarism, and the collecting of memories of the words and actions of the Messiah Jesus that were to constitute the composition materials of the writings of the New Testament.

So at the foot of the Cross, we do not find Peter, but the women—in disbelief, frightened, but present—and among them, the Magdalene is on the front line.

The male disciple or the female disciple he loved?

The Gospel of John is somewhat singular for being different from the synoptic gospels. It describes three women at the foot of the Cross: Mary, the mother of Jesus; Mary the wife of Cleophas; and Mary Magdalene.

"Near the Cross of Jesus stood his mother and his mother's sister, Mary the wife of Clopas, and Mary of Magdala. Seeing his mother and the disciple he loved standing near her, Jesus said to his mother, 'Woman, this is your son.' Then to the disciple he said, 'This is your mother.' And from that moment the disciple made a place for her in his home." (John 19:25-27)

In this narrative setting of striking theological content, the mother of Jesus is present at the Cross as a sign of continuity between the ancient people of Israel and the new community of believers, represented here by the "favorite disciple" to whom she is consigned. In this highly symbolic scene, motherhood and sonship assume spiritual meanings of mutual love and reciprocal recognition. Kinship and discipleship meet and intersect. Mary from Nazareth becomes at once mother and daughter of the Christian community. "And from that moment the disciple made a place for her in his home." (John 19:27)

Traditionally, the enigmatic figure of the "beloved disciple" was identified with the apostle John. Some scholars think it might be a collective figure. Others including Maria Luisa Rigato advance the hypothesis that it indicates

Mary Magdalene herself, for the personal relationship she had with Jesus, a relationship, as we will see, that is pointed to in other texts—the apocryphal and the Gnostic gospels.

Around her—as a guarantor of faith and the founding of the community—could have been created the transmission of memory that lies at the origin of the Fourth Gospel, suggests the theologist Ramon K. Jusino in his article *Mary Magdalene: Author of the Fourth Gospel?* (1998). Following this hypothesis, she would be "the disciple whom Jesus loved" and the one who was at the table during the last supper, reclining next to him. "The disciple Jesus loved was reclining next to Jesus" (John 13:23). The participation of women at the last supper would be an obvious fact, seeing it could not be explained why they should be excluded during the meal, and seeing they were an active presence in the itinerant life of the group, "following and serving". In addition, the different and not entirely compatible versions of the institution of the Eucharist in the synoptic gospels refer less to the detailed account of a historical event than they do to a horizon of salvation represented by Jesus offering his life as a gift to everyone, women and men. (See in this regard the book *Il grande racconto della Bibbia* by Piero Stefani, published in 2017, in particular page 444.) In the Book of John, we see a significant absence of the account of the institution of the Eucharist. It is substituted by the narration of Jesus washing his disciples' feet (John 13:1-20), which reveals its profound meaning: the community will need to distinguish itself in the service of reciprocal love in the same way that Jesus indicated by loving others and offering himself to them until he died, a road that he called upon all his disciples, men and women, to follow.

The interpretative suggestions relayed here are evidently hypotheses, yet they are supported by the surprising qualitative presence of female protagonists in the Gospel of John: the mother, the Samaritan woman, Mary and Martha from Bethany, and the Magdalene. They could imply that women played a meaningful role within the community; that perhaps the memories and stories linked to their experience with Jesus were handed down orally; and that they contributed to the founding of the Johannine Community that lies at the base of the Gospel of John.

To not push too far beyond exegetical tradition, we could accept that the "beloved disciple" is a symbolic and idealized figure who represents the "perfect disciple". The sex of this person is therefore indifferent. It is she or he who, empowered by experiencing a close bond with Jesus, followed him, listened to his teachings, was present at the moment of his death, became a guarantor of faith in his resurrection and an authoritative interpreter of the command for reciprocal love within the "new family of disciplehood inclusive of men and women", which surpasses all established male authority, as stated in the book "*Dio nessuno lo ha mai visto*", *una guida al vangelo di Giovanni* by Pius-Ramon Tragan and Marinella Perroni (2017).

The empty tomb and the apparitions

The memories of the disciples, including the women who followed Jesus, were merged into the different written renditions that gave origin to the gospels. The results differ according to who transmitted them and according to the specific situations of the reference groups.

The accounts of the Passion are highly diverse, and refer to a twofold experience: the discovery of the empty tomb and the post-Resurrection appearances of Jesus, but not always do they converge on the role that the individual characters are carrying out and the emotions they are feeling.

Yet in all the Resurrection reports, women are presented as the first witnesses of the empty tomb, where they had gone to take care of the body of Jesus with oil and perfume.

Mary Magdalene, at the head of the female group, is described as having different types of behavior. In Mark, she flees trembling, along with Mary (the mother of James) and Salome, bewildered by apparitions of angels that testify to the resurrection, and said nothing to anyone (Mark 16:1-8). In Matthew, along with "the other Mary", she recognizes the Risen One and runs to announce this to the other disciples (Matthew 28:1-8). In Luke, her testimony is not considered reliable (Luke 24:1-12). John, more than the others, gives her particular attention and places her at the center of faith in the Risen One, with whom she has an encounter of great emotive impact.

The fourth evangelist, by saying "Meanwhile Mary stayed outside near the tomb, weeping" (John 20:11), underlines how she remained alone crying in front of the empty tomb, distressed by the absence of the body she had loved and lost. She does not know where the dead body of Jesus might be. Only when she hears her name being called is she able to recognize the voice of her Teacher, who has appeared in the garden and seems to be a gardener.

*

"Jesus said, 'Mary!' She turned round then and said
to him in Hebrew, 'Rabbuni!'—which means Master.
Jesus said to her, 'Do not cling to me, because I have not
yet ascended to the Father. But go to the brothers, and
tell them: I am ascending to my Father and your Father,
to my God and your God.' So Mary of Magdala told the
disciples, 'I have seen the Lord,' and that he had said
these things to her." (John 20:16-18)

This narration is a potent symbolic reference to the
search for a loved one who is lost, found and held fast, as
celebrated in the *Song of Songs* (3:1-4), which acts as a
backdrop to this dramatic and impassioned encounter,
much represented in the art made in subsequent centuries.

Here, Mary Magdalene incarnates the ideal type of disciple who sees, recognizes, witnesses and announces. The
Risen One appears to her personally, and avoiding to be
held back, he sends her as a witness of the Living One to
the community of disciples who had become her brethren.
We find here a true apostolic mandate.

A female apostle of Christ

In the encounter of faith with the Risen One, Mary
Magdalene becomes an apostle of Christ, sent by him to
the disciples including Peter, to announce the resurgence
event of which she is a witness and guarantor.

This tradition present in the Johannine Community

gives space to female apostleship in an effective way, and finds its most vigorous representation in the figure of Mary Magdalene. However, it does not constitute a convincing line of thought in the Christian groups that take the upper hand, as they are not much disposed to accept that a woman was the first to receive the apparition of the Risen One.

The Johannine Community had to account for the authority of Peter and with his guidance, legitimized by the groups that referred to the evangelists Matthew and Luke. In Mary Magdalene are present the constitutional elements of being an apostle, in addition to the broader ones "by calling" indicated by Paul the Apostle—having seen the Lord resurrected and having been specially chosen to preach the good news (Epistle to the Romans 1:1)—and the more restricted ones described by Luke: having been a direct witness of Jesus's life, "we must therefore choose someone who has been with us the whole time that the Lord Jesus was travelling round with us" (Acts 1:21), yet she is not part of the apostolic succession.

For this reason, neither her name nor that of the other women are mentioned on the list of the six apparitions compiled by Paul. The apostle reproduces a tradition he has received, different from the Johannine one, and in which female apostles are absent.

"The tradition I handed on to you in the first place, a tradition which I had myself received, was that Christ [. . .] appeared to Cephas; and later to the Twelve; and next he appeared to more than five hundred of the brothers at the same time, most of whom are still with us, though some have fallen asleep; then he appeared to James, and then to all the apostles. Last of all he appeared to me too, as though I was a child born abnormally." (I Corinthians 15:3-8)

Different from the gospels, Paul sanctions Peter as the first to receive the apparitions and ignores the women and Mary Magdalene. This is proof of the competition present in the groups trying to legitimate the authority of their reference figures. In the book *Pietro—Il primo degli apostoli* (2018), the author Claudio Gianotto writes that the groups "aspired to be recognized as the authentic heirs of Jesus and his work". Mary Magdalene was expulsed from the apostolic succession, which became a male prerogative.

"But as she has too little consistence to preach, as her sex is too weak to perform, it is to men that the function of evangelizing is handed over." (*Commentary on the Gospel according to Luke* by Ambrose, Fourth century A.D.).[4]

These clear words of Saint Ambrose express the fragility, lack of authority, and unsuitability of women for missionary and apostolic tasks. In the end, the Magdalene was none other than "a half-frantic woman" as she is described by Celsus in *A True Discourse*, which accuses Christians of placing their faith on the credulousness of "some stupid women".

"Who beheld this? [refers to the Risen One] A half-frantic woman, as you state, and some other one, perhaps, of those who were engaged in the same system of delusion, who had either dreamed so, owing to a peculiar state of mind, or under the influence of a wandering imagination had formed to himself an appearance according to his own wishes, which has been the case with numberless individuals; or, which is most probable, one who desired to impress others with this portent, and by such a falsehood to furnish an occasion to impostors like himself" (Origen, *Against Celsus*, Book II, Chapter LV).[5]

Even pagans like Celsus discredited women and Mary Magdalene, but she and her rivalry with Peter were not consigned to oblivion. Traces of them remain in Gnostic literature.

The communities partaking in the first phases of nascent Christianity were of different provenances and sensibilities. They were often in conflict with one another regarding the identity that the new religious reality based on the message of Jesus of Nazareth needed to assume. One of the issues that constituted a subject of debate and polemics was the role of women. It was no surprise that several of these groups, distinguished by the lively presence of significant female figures, were accused of being heretic by other communities belonging to the Great Church that was being structured according to the cultural models of the surrounding patriarchal society.

In this direction are oriented, for instance, the pastoral epistles (to Timothy and to Titus), where the second-generation disciples of Paul the Apostle indicate the subordinate manner in which women must behave, renouncing the forms of female leadership that were emerging in a number of communities in Asia Minor. This is evident in the apocryphal story *Acts of Paul and Thecla*, written in the second century. While the disciple Thecla baptizes and preaches, the exhortations in the First Epistle to Timothy follow an entirely different line. "During instruction, a woman should be quiet and respectful. I am not giving permission for a woman to teach or to tell a man what to do. A woman ought not to speak." (I Timothy 2:11-12)[6]

Perhaps because of the growing exclusion of women from leading roles, many followers of Mary Magdalene found acceptance in the communities that acknowledged the importance of her being the recipient of the revelation of the Risen Christ. Indeed, in an overall picture of divergent, variegated and complex circumstances, the second century ushered in the spreading of the Gnostic movement to which many Christian groups adhered that desired to travel the roads of knowledge (*gnosis*) and wisdom (*sophia*). Women were the undisputed protagonists of the Gnostic phenomenon, and their writings "are part of the most important testimonies of a memory of Mary Magdalene," says Cristina Simonelli in *An Apostle between Spirituality and Conflict*, Part 2 of the book *Mary of Magdala: Revisiting the Sources*. Several communities such as the Naassenes, for instance, claimed to have been taught their doctrines by Mariamne, a variant of the name Mary Magdalene. (Hippolytus of Rome wrote about this in *Refutation of All Heresies*, Book V, Chapter 7:1. And Origen wrote about it in *Against Celsus*, Book V, Chapter 15:62).

What the codices of Nag Hammadi say

The Gnostic texts, written between the second and fourth centuries, and only partly recovered thanks to the discovery of the Nag Hammadi library in 1945, reveal the importance of the role of women; it is emphasized by the centrality of the first woman apostle and by the mise-en-scène of her conflict with Peter. This reflects a much broader contrast between the proto-orthodox communities and the Christian groups that chose to present other traditions regarding Jesus that had remained secret (apocryphal) and hidden to most people. In some of these texts, knowledge of the divine mysteries, which was reserved for an elite within a restricted circle, is legitimized by the teachings of Mary Magdalene as an interpreter and revealer of the Gnostic doctrine where *gnosis* indicates a spiritual process that leads to knowledge and awareness. On this religious horizon, the center of the message is focused on the ignorance from which individuals must free themselves by discovering within themselves the wisdom and divine light effused by the Teacher.

The figure of Mary Magdalene that is present in the Gnostic writings—many of which describe traditions that go back to the era of the canonical gospels of the New Testament—is not enriched by biographical details, which are entirely absent; rather she emerges as an influential symbol of knowledge, to the degree that, as the disciple and companion of Jesus, she reveals his hidden wisdom.

In the Gospel of Peter (mid-second century), which is defined by the scholar Montague Rhodes James as "the earliest uncanonical account of the Passion that exists," the Magdalene appears with her women friends as they are on their way to the sepulcher. She is presented as "a discipless of the Lord" (12:50) by the rare use of the Greek feminine form *mathētria* of the term "disciple" (masculine: *mathētēs*).

The Gospel of Mary (mid-second century), which refers authoritatively to her important role by naming her in the title, reveals the existence of oral traditions regarding Mary Magdalene that were probably later combined in the written gospels. This means we are looking at transmissions of the spoken word that could go back either to the experience of the "beloved disciple" who had established intimate and profound communication with the Risen One, or to stories handed down by women who were witnesses and custodians of the memory of Jesus's message, from Galilee to the Resurrection, as Carla Ricci upholds in her book *Maria Maddalena: L'amata di Gesù nei testi apocrifi* (2017).

The Gospel of Mary indicates her role as a mediator between Jesus and the disciples. Faced with the distress of the men frightened by the words of the Risen One who walks away from them after having exhorted them to go forth and preach, Mary Magdalene reacts powerfully, comforting them and encouraging them to overcome their faint-heartedness.

"Then Mary stood up, greeted them all, and said to her brethren, 'Do not weep and do not grieve nor be irresolute, for his grace will be entirely with you and will protect you. But rather, let us praise his greatness, for he has prepared us and made us into men.'

When Mary said this, she turned their hearts to the

Good, and they began to discuss the words of the Savior. Peter said to Mary, 'Sister we know that the Savior loved you more than the rest of women. Tell us the words of the Savior which you remember—which you know, but we do not, nor have we heard them.' Mary answered and said, 'What is hidden from you I will proclaim to you.'" (Gospel of Mary 9:12–10:8)

But the disciples, though they were aware that Mary Magdalene was able to reveal the Lord's thought, are loath to accept that he prefers a woman to them. Skepticism and irritation ensue as they listen to her words, which seem to regard teachings that are different from the ones they received.

"But Andrew answered and said to the brethren, 'Say what you wish to say about what she has said. I at least do not believe that the Savior said this. For certainly these teachings are strange ideas.'" (Gospel of Mary 17:10-15)

Not only Andrew but also Peter is jealous of the privileges that the Teacher gave her. He too has difficulty accepting that a woman be singled out for secrets of which he knows nothing, and that she issue detailed teachings of Jesus.

"Peter answered and spoke concerning these same things. He questioned them about the Savior: 'Did he really speak with a woman without our knowledge and not openly? Are we to turn about and all listen to her? Did he prefer her to us?'" (Gospel of Mary 17:16-22)

But Levi defends Mary Magdalene, recognizing in her Jesus's "favorite disciple," seeing how "he loved her more than us."

"Then Mary wept and said to Peter: 'My brother Peter, what do you think? Do you think that I thought this up myself in my heart, or that I am lying about the Savior?' Levi answered and said to Peter, 'Peter you have always been hot-tempered. Now I see you contending against the woman like the adversaries. But if the Savior made her worthy, who are you indeed to reject her? Surely the Savior knows her very well. That is why he loved her more than us. Rather let us be ashamed and put on the perfect man, and acquire him for ourselves as he commanded us, and preach the gospel, not laying down any other rule or other law beyond what the Savior said.'" (Gospel of Mary 18:5-21)

This Gnostic text manifests an open contrast with the official Church regarding the role of women, specifically regarding the recognition of Mary Magdalene's authority. Furthermore, she is presented as the type of perfect Gnostic who imparts teachings she received from Jesus, including the one related to the ascension of the soul purified of all natural elements, a central, widespread question in certain currents of Gnostic thought.

In the Gospel of Philip (second century), three women

are mentioned (all by the name of Mary) who accompany Jesus.

"There were three who always walked with the Lord: Mary his mother, and her sister, and the Magdalene, the one who was called his companion (*koinonos*). His sister and his mother and his companion were each a Mary." (Gospel of Philip 59:6-11)

Mary Magdalene is attributed with the special status of Jesus's companion/partner and this gives her standing among the disciples.

"And the companion of the [savior is] Mary Magdalene. [The savior loved] her more than [all] the disciples, [and used to] kiss her [often] on her [mouth]. The rest of [the disciples]. They said to him, 'Why do you love her more than all of us?' The savior answered and said to them, 'Why do I not love you like her? When a blind man and one who sees are both together in darkness, they are no different from one another. When the light comes, then he who sees will see the light, and he who is blind will remain in darkness.'" (Gospel of Philip 63:34—64:10).

This excerpt shows clearly the great intimacy between Jesus and Mary Magdalene. According to Gnostic language and thought, this union is to be interpreted in a spiritual and not sexual sense, because it refers to the "mystical union" (syzygy) between heavenly wisdom (*sophia*) and

Christ (*logos*) sealed by the kiss, a sign of greeting and a metaphor of the alliance between the two, and of their mutual spiritual nurturing, in addition to being an initiation rite through which knowledge and wisdom is given.

Moreover, light is shone on the motive of the predilection for Mary Magdalene compared to the other disciples: Mary is able to see the Light and welcome it, contrary to the men, who remain in the dark. Her capacity for listening and comprehending makes her a leader and a spiritual authority.

Also in the Gospel of Thomas (probably from the second century), a collection of 114 sayings attributed to Jesus, Mary runs counter to a particularly misogynist Peter.

"Simon Peter said to them, 'Let Mary leave us, for women are not worthy of life.' Jesus said, 'I myself shall lead her in order to make her male, so that she too may become a living spirit resembling you males. For every woman who will make herself male will enter the kingdom of heaven.'" (Gospel of Thomas 114)

To the refusal of Peter who wants to make the Magdalene leave because she is a woman, Jesus replies by indicating how in perfection there is an annulment of opposites (high and low; outside and inside; male and female— Gospel of Thomas 22), meaning that he will transform feminine weakness (a metaphor for the creaturely condition) into masculine strength, a symbol of spiritual reality. Both women and men are called upon to turn into spiritual beings and become Living Spirits.

Mary Magdalene and the group of female disciples

Pistis Sophia (second half of the third century) or *Book of the Savior* is a Gnostic gospel containing secret revelations by Jesus addressed to the disciples gathered in assembly with Mary Magdalene, Mary the mother, and Martha from Bethany, the "female disciples" (*mathetriai*).[7] It is significant that the text presents the Twelve as a mixed group composed of eight men and four women (Chapter 7 and following), as further proof of the fact that women too, like men, are depositories of the revelation and responsible for its transmission.

Women's inclusion is also made explicit in *The Sophia of Jesus Christ* (written between the second and third centuries), where the group of seven women is added to the twelve disciples in a story that evokes the episode of their commissioning during the apparition in Galilee (Gospel of Matthew 28:16-20).

The *Pistis Sophia* shows the Magdalene as the favorite disciple of all, she who poses most of the questions (over 67 of them) in a brisk dialogue with the Risen One, and she who best understands the message of the Teacher. He lauds her on more than one occasion. "Mariam, thou blessed one, whom I will complete in all the mysteries of the height, speak openly, thou art she whose heart is more directed to the Kingdom of Heaven than all thy brothers" (Chapter 17). In this gospel too, her protagonism is disliked by the disciples, and by Peter in particular, all of whom feel one-upped by her and her questions. "Peter leapt forward, he said to Jesus: 'My Lord, we are not able to suffer this woman who takes the opportunity from us, and does not allow anyone of us to speak, but she speaks many times" (Chapter 36). But it is not only a question of having a quick wit and possessing lively curiosity. Often the disciples do not understand, and Mary Magdalene, who better comprehends, interprets and discerns, must intervene to explain (Chapter 94). She symbolizes knowledge (gnosis) and as such she is the bride and priestess of Jesus, a role that males such as Peter could not accept.

> "Mariam came forward. She said: 'My Lord, my mind is understanding at all times that I should come forward at any time and give the interpretation of the words which she [the *Pistis Sophia*] spoke, but I am afraid of Peter, for he threatens me and he hates our race.'" (Chapter 72).

Evidently, this gospel, too, expresses through the conflict with Peter the lively debate on the role that women could take on in the communities, and on who should legitimately guide those communities.

The *Pistis Sophia* offers a particularly meaningful answer to Peter's complaints, since Jesus himself joins the debate, exhorting Mariam and the women benevolently to "Give way to the men, your brothers, that they may question also," and confirming that everyone who will be filled with the spirit of light—female or male—can have the task of interpreting his words. "No one will be able to prevent it." Therefore, women—and Mary Magdalene represents them worthily—are by no means excluded from knowledge, perfection, or from occupying places of authoritative guidance.

In several contexts, she is presented as a figure who spurs the discouraged apostles. "Be a messenger for me to those lost orphans. Make haste rejoicing, and go unto the Eleven," recites a Coptic text written in the fourth century (the Manichaean Psalm Book, the Psalms of Heracleides), indicating her as "a net-caster" and the one who incites the disciples to persevere in their missionary work.[8]

Again it is she in the *Hymn 40, on the Resurrection* by the poet Romanos the Melodist, who wakens her sleeping friends, exhorting Peter and John to persevere and not lose heart. With the other myrrh-bearing women, she rouses the apostles to action. "Why so downhearted? Why cover your faces? Lift up your hearts, Christ is risen. Stand in line for the dance, and say with us, 'The Lord is risen.' He who was born before the dawn has shone out, so cease glowering looks, send forth new shoots. Spring is here." (Romanos the Melodist, *On the Resurrection* 22:4-10)[9]

It is surprising that in the sixth century, when this hymn was composed, there is still talk of the conflict between Peter and Mary Magdalene. She, as the apostle of the resurrection, is sent by Jesus to the disciples to reassure them—they must not be upset that the Lord has not become manifest to them first. In relation to the male leadership that criticizes her position of guidance and the legitimacy of her announcement, Mary Magdalene, the representative of the women active in the communities, continues to embody the female right to exercise authority.

In a word, Gnostic literature testifies to the existence of

a widespread tradition related to the apostolic function of Mary Magdalene, and only a few traces of it are preserved in the synoptic gospels, while other more significant elements are found in the Gospel of John. As we already saw, by allowing her to speak, John assigns her the role of a privileged interlocutor (Gospel of John 20:1-18). The movements of Gnostic influence, on the other hand, acknowledge the evangelical tradition, and in different contexts they refer to John's line of thought to propose people who could constitute an alternative to the supremacy of Peter and the circle of the Twelve, with which not all communities identified.

In these Christian groups it was important to be worthy of Jesus's teaching regardless of gender. The women and men who received his word, meaning they were the recipients of the revelation, take on a function of authority in so far as they are responsible for the diffusion of the teaching they have received. The fact that the Twelve were accompanied by a group of women (see *The Sophia of Jesus Christ*) or that they are considered to be a mixed group (see the *Pistis Sophia*) means that women as well as men can receive the revelation and transmit it. Mary Magdalene, a recipient of Jesus's teaching, is a carrier of the apostolic tradition.

Finally, it must be noted that there exists a minor libertine current of the Gnostic movement that authored a blasphemous text named *Questions of Mary* (*Greater and Lesser Questions of Mary*), where it is written that salvation is obtained through sexual union, and where Jesus indicates to Mary his own semen as the way to reach it

(Epiphanius, *Panarion*, 26.8:1-3). The few pieces of information that have reached us through the compendium against heresies composed by Epiphanius, the bishop of Salamis, do not allow us to gain more precise knowledge of this text or to know which community it refers to, but it is interesting to note that here too, Mary Magdalene is a key figure.

The apocryphal Mary

In contrast with the Gnostic texts in which Mary Magdalene is described as the spiritual companion of Christ and as a revealer of knowledge, in the variegated and very complex literature commonly called apocryphal, her figure is confused with the other Marys of the canonical gospels, and with the sinner in Luke 7:37 and following verses. Sometimes she is even substituted with the mother of Jesus in her role as witness of the resurrection.

The *Epistula Apostolorum* (Latin for "Letter of the Apostles") written in the second century describes the Magdalene at the tomb with the sisters from Bethany bewildered and weeping because of Jesus's death. The text says they were called to announce to the apostles that the resurrection had taken place.

"And as they mourned and wept, the Lord showed himself unto them and said to them: 'For whom weep ye? Weep no more. I am he whom ye seek. But let one of you go to your brethren and say: Come ye, the Master is risen from the dead.'" (*Epistula Apostolorum*, 10:1).[10]

First Martha, then Mary Magdalene go, but the men remain incredulous and no one has faith in the words of the women. "None of them believed me that you are alive," Mary says to the Lord. Only the direct contact of Peter, Thomas and Andrew with the Lord's wounds convinces the apostles.

In the *Acts of Pilate*, also known as the *Gospel of Nicodemus* (fifth century), the apostle Mary Magdalene is with the mother of Jesus and with Joseph of Arimathea at the moment of crucifixion. She retains her active role of denunciation and proclaims her will to go to Rome to see the emperor in order to publicly condemn the unjust death of Jesus.

Other texts, from the area around Egypt (the Gospel of Gamaliel, and the *Book of the Resurrection of Jesus Christ* by Bartholomew the Apostle—from the fourth to sixth century) substitute the Magdalene with Mary the mother of Jesus, to whom the Risen One appears and who takes on increasing importance in Christian narration. No longer is it the beloved disciple who weeps over the death of her teacher and who is invested with the mission to announce his resurrection, but Jesus's mother occupies the stage and takes on a new and different centrality in the ecclesiastical and religious experience.

"And Jesus said to her: 'O Mary, you have wept sufficiently. [. . .] O Mary, recognise my glory; look, I am comforting you with the words of life, be not ashamed therefore, nor afraid. Look at my face, O my mother, and you will recognise me [. . .] It is I, Jesus over whom you are weeping, who is now comforting you at the beginning of His resurrection.' [. . .] And Jesus said to her: 'Go in haste[11] and announce my resurrection from the dead to my brethren. Go in haste, O my mother, leave this place and do not stand at the right side of my tomb.'" (Gospel of Gamaliel/Lament of Mary).

And Jesus's mother actually confirms Peter as the leader of the community.

"And Peter said unto Mary, 'Thou that are highly favored, entreat the Lord that he would reveal unto us the things that are in the heavens.' And Mary said unto Peter, 'O stone hewn out of the rock, did not the Lord build his church upon thee? Go thou therefore first and ask him.' Peter saith again, 'O tabernacle that art spread abroad.' Mary saith, 'Thou art the image of Adam.' (*Book of the Resurrection* 4:1-5)[12]

In some Gnostic communities she was symbolically authoritative, but as the Great Church established itself, the figure of Mary Magdalene became subject to misrepresentation and reduction, and was replaced with the mother of Jesus, whose cult became strongly dominant within Christianity.

Paul does not even mention the Magdalene among the witnesses of the resurrection (I Corinthians 15:5). The function of apostle became a male prerogative and the authoritative exercise of the missionary commitment was recognized neither to women nor to Mary Magdalene, whose identity took on other characteristics more in line with the female models presented to the communities of believers.

Despite the dismissal of the Gnostic literature that had reserved a major place for her, the interest for Mary Magdalene did not wane over the course of time. Since the fourth century, her cult was established in the Orient at the ancient Greek city of Ephesus, where it was said she arrived with the Virgin Mary and Saint John, and where her tomb was venerated. Easter liturgies on the so-called "Sunday of the myrrh-bearers" commemorated the Magdalene and the sainted women who had gone to the sepulcher with scented oil to take care of Jesus's corpse. From the Byzantine synaxaria, we know that July 22 was dedicated to a holiday in her name that moved West in the eighth century.

On many occasions, the fathers of the Church reflect upon Mary Magdalene with acuity and psychological sensitivity, albeit not without a certain dose of ambiguity, which is partly due to their being sensible interpreters of the message of Christ in cultural contexts sometimes far from the Teacher of Galilee's original environment. And partly it is due to the assumption in their thought of several prejudices of the patriarchal societies in which they lived. Although their spiritual and moral considerations open onto spaces of parity by recognizing the apostolate of the Magdalene, they have nonetheless had no bearing on a juridic level, not allowing women to have an equally legitimate ministerial function.

The great misunderstanding: sinner

The early Christian writers consider Mary Magdalene to be the first witness of the resurrection (Irenaeus, *Against Heresies* Book 5, Chapter 31:1-2). They underline how her faith is given by love (Tertullian, *Against Praxeas* 25:2) and they proclaim her "apostle of the apostles" (Hippolytus of Rome, *Commentary on the Song of Songs* 25:6). But such elements of recognition that single her out for her role as an authentic disciple started to diminish to the degree in which the limits attributed to the female gender emerged. We have seen how Ambrose, for instance, considered her womanly "weakness" as the reason she could not be as full an apostle as the men, who thereby preserved their leadership and superiority (Ambrose of Milan, *Commentary on the Gospel according to Luke* 10:165).

Hippolytus of Rome believes that Mary Magdalene compensates for the fall of Eve, a comparison readily amplified by other authors. Gregory of Nyssa affirms how contrary to Eve, who had brought ruin to humanity with her disobedience, the Magdalene repaired the overthrow by becoming to men the guide to faith (*Against Eunomius*, Book 12). For Ambrose too, she is the "new Eve," a liberatress and repairer of the female sex (*Concerning Virginity*

4:20). Cyril of Alexandria emphasizes the typological antithesis by asserting that "the gospel of salvation was given to the woman [Magdalene], who was once the minister of death [Eve]" (*Comment on the Gospel of John*, 20:17). Women needed more grace than men, and just as Eve induced Adam to sin, so had Mary Magdalene repelled the cause of evil with the vision of the Risen One (*Commentary on the Book of the Prophet Isaiah* 27:11). Augustine of Hippo is even more incisive: *Per feminam mors, per feminam vita* ("From a woman, death came, from a woman, life." Sermon 232, 2:2). Tradition would reserve this contrast predominantly for the Virgin Mary, the most eminently anti-Eve.

In this way, Christian writers propose again the contrast between a negative symbol of femininity represented by the first woman who brought death into the world, and the positive model of the disciple Magdalene.

As Romanos the Melodist affirms in *Hymn 40*: "For what has come to pass was divine disposition, that the women first to fall, should be first to see him resurrected."[13]

And, Gregory the Great developed this redress of the female gender from the fault of Eve even further:

"Since in heaven, it is a woman who has poured out the man [the poison of] death, it is also a woman who, coming from the tomb, announces life to men. And the one that records the words of him who vivifies is the one who brought back the deadly words of the serpent. The Lord seems to want to use not the language of words, but the language of facts, to tell the human race: 'From the hand that handed you the drink of death, yes, from this same hand, receive the cup of life.'" (Homily 25:6)[14]

And he adds that Mary Magdalene, who was present in the garden where the tomb was located, became the first "witness of the divine mercy" (Homily 25:10). Jesus had mercy on her, for she was full of irremediable love. He made her recognize him, transformed her tears into joy, and invested her with the role of heraldess of the resurrection.

Despite such delicate introspective analyses, it was foremostly Gregory the Great who generated a fateful interpretative misunderstanding that brought the Western Church to construct a misrepresented and mythic female character.

While in Eastern tradition the image of Mary Magdalene was consolidated around her being a myrrh-bearer and witness of the resurrection, in Western tradition, several identity mix-ups between her and the other women present in the gospels can be noted from the third century onward. Slowly but surely, her role as an apostle was diminished by superimposing the image of the penitent sinner. Perhaps out of the need to harmonize similar stories, different women were unified under the same name as Mary Magdalene. There is the Magdalene freed of the seven demons, which were, however, interpreted as a sign of sinfulness (Mark 16:9; Luke 8:2). There is the anonymous prostitute who wets Jesus's feet with her tears and sprinkles them with perfume (Luke 7:36-50). In the gospel of John, Mary of Bethany is named as the one who anoints the feet of the Nazarene with costly perfume of nard, and then dries them with her hair (John 12:1-8). In the home of Simon the leper, there is the anonymous woman who poured on Jesus's head a "jar of very expensive perfume" (Matthew 26:6-13; Mark 14:3-9).

While Origen (*Commentary on the Gospel of Matthew*, Chapter 26) and Jerome (*Commentary on Matthew*, Chapter 4) communicated their disagreement and perplexity regarding the identification of the women who anointed Jesus, Gregory the Great has no doubts and melds these figures with Mary Magdalene (Homilies 25 and 33). With the weight of his authority, he begins the process of building the identity that over the following centuries would see her no longer as an apostle, but as the quintessential sinner.

> "The one that Luke calls a sinner, and that John names Mary, we believe that she is that Mary of whom, according to Mark, the Lord has cast out seven demons. And what are these seven demons, if not the universality of all vices?" (Gregory the Great, Homily 33)[15]

The tears of the sinner (Luke 7:38) are a sign of intense love, and as such associated with the ones Mary Magdalene cries at the tomb (John 20:11).

All later Latin authors except Paschasius Radbertus, Bernard of Clairvaux and Nicholas of Clairvaux would follow Gregory in this assimilation, which we still find for centuries after in preaching, tracts and art.

Female apostle: a feeble but persistent trace

Mediaeval texts document a variegated portrayal, not at all unitary, of Mary Magdalene perceived in all her complexity. Substantially, it is divided into the three modes expressed by patristic synthesis: she is an apostle, a sinner and a repentant.

In the 11th and 12th centuries, her recognition as the first witness of the resurrection remains alive, as she is defined by Hippolytus of Rome as the "apostle of the apostles" (*Commentary on the Song of Songs*, 25), a formula that remained popular until the late Middle Ages. The philosopher Peter Abelard even emphasizes her role by placing her and the other women "as apostles, yet above the apostles" (Letter 7) and underlines how these women "deserved to be the first to see the glory of his resurrection".[16]

> "She is said to be the apostle of the apostles, that is to say, the herald of the heralds, because the Lord first directed her to the apostles so that she might proclaim the joy of the resurrection to them. [. . .] And she was first to sing proclaiming that which she was first to see. After her, this resurrection joy was given to other women, before it was given to the apostles, to the men." (Peter Abelard)[17]

The use of the title apostle referring to Mary Magdalene is also found in Byzantine literature (Theophanes Kerameus, Homilies 30 and 31) insofar as it is within the classic stereotypes that see her task as messenger as an exception and surpassing of the fragile feminine nature. In Orthodox Christianity, Mary Magdalene is a spiritual figure with strong evangelical traits, without the characteristics of the redeemed sinner.

Several iconographic examples sustain her image as heraldess and preacheress. One miniature in the *Gospel Book of Henry the Lion* (1173-1175) shows her as she advances in front of seven apostles who turn their heads to listen to her. In the Florentine panel painting *Mary Magdalene with Eight Scenes from her Life* (anonymous, around 1280) she teaches women and men authoritatively. To these better-known depictions, we can add the mural painted at the Oratorio di Santa Maria in Valle in the town of Cividale del Friuli. The fresco, called *Santa Maria Maddalena e Santa Sofia con le figlie Carità, Speranza e Fede* (late-12th or early-13th century), shows the Magdalene in a frontal position in an oratorial stance, a rare picture that deviates from traditional iconography (the jar of ointment that normally identifies her is not present) to take on the qualities of an apostle who possesses knowledge.

In some ways, artistic portrayals support the literary testimonies and the preaching, which often dwell on her role as an evangelist. *De Vita Beatae Mariae Magdalenae et sororis ejus Sanctae Marthae* by pseudo-Rabanus Maurus (12th century) highlights her being the chosen witness of the first apparition of the risen Christ, and her assignment as an apostle.

"Indeed she was enriched with multiple signs of divine dignity, inasmuch as through the apparition she

was the first to be lauded; through the honor of the apostolate she was elevated; as the heraldess of the resurrection of Christ she was assigned; and as the prophet of his
ascension to heaven she was chosen for the apostles."

(Pseudo-Rabanus Maurus, *The Life of Saint Mary
Magdalene*, translation from the Italian by Wendy
Wheatley)

Thomas Aquinas also recognizes her as the *apostolorum
apostola*, "apostle of the apostles" (*Commentary on the
Gospel of John*, 20, 2519) insofar as it was her task to
announce the Lord's resurrection to the disciples, which
they in turn would preach to the entire world.

This privilege did not, however, free the theologian from
the Aristotelian prejudice that women were by nature inferior ("a female is an incomplete male," Aristotle believed),
nor did it change the real condition of women in the
medieval Church, for they were not allowed to preach or
teach.

It is interesting to know that thanks to Mary Magdalene, France could boast the apostolic origin of its Church
on the same footing as Rome (with Peter), Byzantium (with
Andrew) and Spain (with James). It was foremostly in
France that romanticized stories about her apostolic life
developed due to the flourishing of "Latin legends" which
from the 11th century spread news about her trip by sea
from Palestine to the South of France; about the transport
of relics from the original tomb in Ephesus to Provence;
and a series of miraculous stories.

These narrations as well as the monastic liturgies that

were taking on more solid forms at the time favored increasing devotion to the Magdalene. The Benedictine monastery in Vézelay, Burgundy was the first recognized center of worship of Mary Magdalene in the West. Abbot Geoffroy, elected in 1037 and the founder of the reformed Benedictine order of Cluny, claimed to hold the relics of Mary Magdalene, the saint under whose patronage he had placed the monastery, and he established a surprising devotional practice. In 1058, Pope Stephen IX confirmed the existence of her tomb in Vézelay, which became an important place of pilgrimage for a good two centuries until the discovery of other mortal remains of the Magdalene by rival Provençal monks in 1279 in the crypt of Saint-Maximin-la-Sainte-Baume, about 40 kilometers west of Aix-en-Provence. These monks were given regal patronage by Charles II, the Angevin king of Sicily (later King of Naples) and by Boniface VIII, who confirmed the authenticity of the relics and thereby favored the arising of sanctuaries dedicated to Mary Magdalene.

The mendicant orders took her as a hagiographic reference model, particularly the Dominicans, who were on a mission to convert the Cathars, a Christian religious sect with Gnostic beliefs deemed heretical by the Roman Catholic Church. The Cathars venerated Mary Magdalene, and the Dominicans placed themselves under her protection. In this way, the saint became functional to the needs of orthodoxy in the Western Church.

The lively construction of legends and numerous hagiographic texts in Latin and in vernacular flourished in Europe, finding compilation in the book *The Golden*

Legend (*Legenda aurea* in Latin) by the Dominican Jacobus de Voragine (1228-1298), where ample space is dedicated to the episodes that took place upon Mary Magdalene's arrival in France along with Martha, Lazarus and the bishop Maximinus of Aix. Mary Magdalene, presented as "born of most noble parents" and "enormously wealthy," is the apostle who preached the Gospel of Christ in Marseille "with great single-mindedness."

> "Everyone there admired her for her beauty, for her eloquence, and for her sweet manner of speaking. And it is no wonder that the lips which had pressed kisses so loving and so tender on our Lord's feet should breathe the perfume of the word of God more copiously than others." (Jacobus de Voragine, *The Golden Legend* volume 4, *The Life of Saint Mary Magdalene*)[18]

With her words, Mary Magdalene did not only dissuade the people who sacrificed to idols, but led the pagan prince and his wife to the Christian faith, and with them the entire city of Marseille. Her role as an apostle and preacheress is narrated with vigor and the memory of it is still preserved in the fresco by Gaudenzio Ferrari, *The Baptism of the Princes of Marseille* (around 1475-1546).

In *The Golden Legend*, Mary Magdalene is definitely identified as the sinner of the gospel. By means of a refined play of substitutions, she becomes a repentant who wishes to lead a life of hermithood, and retreats into a cave in the same way as Saint Mary of Egypt, the legendary prostitute who as a sign of repentance lived in the desert. On her model, part of the romanticized story of Mary Magdalene is developed. Closing the story of her life as a recluse is the narration of the angels who bring her to heaven every day to listen to the celestial choir.

The images of sinner and repentant are layered over the memory of the apostle, diminishing her ecclesiastic role—a process that was facilitated by art. The pictorial cycle found in the Magdalene Chapel in Assisi (Basilica inferiore di San Francesco d'Assisi) is, for instance, greatly effective in this regard. Called *Storie della Maddalena* and made at the workshop of Giotto, the painting refers to *The Golden Legend* in its evangelical elements (supper in the house of the Pharisee, the resurrection of Lazarus, the crucifixion, the resurrection and *Noli me tangere*) and in its legendary elements (her landing in Marseille, her life as a hermit, and her being brought to heaven by the angels). These iconographic models were joined by the portrait of the Magdalene in accordance with the stereotypes that were to remain for centuries in our collective imagination: long blond hair and red dress indicating licentiousness; kneeling position indicating repentance; bodily vicinity to Christ indicating unwillingness to take leave of her loved one; emaciated physical appearance indicating redemption for her past existence as a sinner.

The repentant's irremediable love

The repentant Mary Magdalene became the patroness of the eremitic movement as a model of ascesis and escape from the world, an example of the guiltiness of humankind, an instance of divine compassion. Precisely because she was the ideal figure for conversion, she became one of the most popular saints for the mediaeval believer who wished for reform and redemption. "To sin is to convert" went the saying that fed the piety of the mendicant orders (Franciscans and Dominicans), the creators of a vast body of religious literature, and of the pauperism-related and reformatory movements that saw in her the symbol of a sinning Church in need of salvation.

Francesco d'Assisi (Saint Francis) enjoyed going to pray at an oratory in Fonte Colombo, Rieti dedicated to Mary Magdalene, whom he upheld as an example of mortification and poverty. The "penitents of Assisi" as the Franciscans used to be called at the beginning, chose her and John the Baptist as icons of penitence. In particular, Francis and his devotion to the Passion of Christ favored the mysticism of the cross and the amorous contemplation that find their model emblematically in the figure of Mary Magdalene.

Also the Dominicans have always shown special interest for her, and she is one of the order's patron saints. The friars rooted their life in her love for Christ and in her preaching. Several women linked to the order, such as Catherine of Siena, were devoted to her as to a mother and a safe guide. Many convents have been named after Mary Magdalene, and the Dominicans have taken guardianship over the places of worship dedicated to her in the South of France.

While Mary Magdalene is an icon of contemplative life, at

the same time she has become a model for people working at the service of charity for the redemption of women who have succumbed to sin. For this reason, prostitutes became a motive of attention on behalf of several men of faith, who in the rehabilitation of these women read the possibility to become the subject of redemption and signs of benevolence from God. Robert of Arbrissel was one of the first preachers to take care of prostitutes, gather them in houses and submit them to religious discipline, but Rudolf of Worms was the one who founded the Order of Magdalenes in Rhineland, approved by Gregory IX in 1227 for the women's reformation. Cloistered communities of "Magdalenes" began to spread, aiming at the protection and rehabilitation of prostitutes. In 1376, Pope Gregory XI officially recognized the Repentant Sisters of Saint Mary Magdalene, and clearly defined the institutional aspects of these foundations that were multiplying all across Europe. Numerous orders, convents, confraternities, conservatories and refuges dedicated to her were established in the Middle Ages and during the entire modern age, proving how the saint was viewed as a protectress of poor, marginalized and lost young women.

As an emblematic figure of conversion and redemption, the saint became a model to imitate. See Margaret of Cortona, given the name Nova Magdalena by Benedict XIII for having gone from a life of sin to an existence of mortification marked by a very human love for Jesus. Of particular interest is one vision in which Christ himself points out to Margaret the example of Mary Magdalene, including her among the "pure virgins" after the Madonna and Catherine the Martyr of Alexandria (Lodovico da Pelago, *Antica Leggenda della vita e de' miracoli di Santa Margherita di Cortona*, V).

In an increasingly considerable manner, the story of this repentant woman became the stuff of sermons, treaties on penitence, and sacred representations of a popular nature. Spiritual dramas, born from the antiphon of the Easter liturgy, exited the confines of church walls in the 13th century to become spectacles for the people, enriched with dramatic flourishes and imaginary details that could easier make an impression on the sensitivity of the devoted.

During the 14th, 15th and 16th centuries, representations of the Passion were performed on town squares to encourage the faithful to change their life. The element of conversion became more and more important; emphasis was placed not only on Mary Magdalene being a converted sinner, but especially on the impassioned love that had led her to follow Jesus until his death. The cruel elements of the Passion, derived from apocryphal gospels or highly popular texts such as *Meditations on the Life of Christ* by pseudo-Bonaventure, were impressed with an emotional impact on the public, which participated dramatically in the events surrounding the death of Christ. With this theatricalization of episodes from the Bible, an attempt was made to get the faithful to enter the stage, arouse their compassion and induce them to identify. In the sacred representations, the female characters stood out as positive models, for instance empathy for those inflicted with pain (Veronica), faithfulness (the pious women), undying love (Mary Magdalene), and strong motherhood marked by sorrow (Mary). Like the mother of Jesus, these women represent all suffering humanity, or like Magdalene, show the ability to redeem themselves through love.

Figurative art was greatly influenced by this interpretation. See the Mary Magdalene portrayed standing with her arms dramatically stretched toward the skies in a gesture of pain (Cimabue, *Crucifixion*, around 1277-1283), kneeling at the foot of the Cross (Giotto, *Crucifixion*, around 1303-1305), or prostrate on the ground (Niccolò di Pietro Gerini, *Crucifixion*, around 1395-1400).

As for Masaccio, in his *Crucifixion* (1426), he intensifies Mary Magdalene's distress even more by painting her from behind with her back bent and arms wide, imbuing her with intense and tragic expressivity. Such communicational force is found in Mourning of Christ paintings and representations of The Piety, where the suffering mother is joined by the despair of Mary Magdalene as an icon of the immeasurable pain of those who have lost a loved one. Atrocious interior torment is made manifest by agitated, desperate shouting in *Compianto sul Cristo morto* (around 1463-1490) by Niccolò dell'Arca, and in the *Lamentation* depictions by Guido Mazzoni sculpted between 1475 and 1492 in Busseto, Modena, Ferrara, Cremona, Venice and Naples.

But grief for the death of Jesus is not sufficient to redeem a life marked by sin, and here the image of the hermit mortified by fasting and penitence came to the fore. Donatello (particularly in his aforementioned *Penitent Magdalene* sculpture) masterfully depicts an ageing, emaciated woman enveloped only by long, matted hair. Her hands are joined in prayer, and the posture of her body is marked by detachment from worldly things.

Mary Magdalene thus became a symbol of the human possibility of redemption. In some way, in a complex strat-ification of imagery, it summarizes the ambiguity of wom-anhood, because she is condemned to having to surpass its limits, becoming the patroness of the penitential female movement of the Late Middle Ages.

While the Middle Ages bequeathed to the modern age a complex, multifaceted Mary Magdalene, the Renaissance in turn enriched her personality with particular sensitivity. The humanists' new historical and philological comprehension cast doubt on the traditional identity of Jesus's disciple, calling into question the typical interpretational canons of the Scriptures. At the same time, a more direct reading of the holy text by women allowed for broader considerations.

Women's approach

On several occasions, women's writing, which matured between the 12th and 16th centuries, took the women in the gospels as its subject matter, especially Mary Magdalene. She is perceived as a model of perseverance and humility, or, to quote Catherine of Siena, "the sweet apostle in love" who embraces the Cross and is inebriated by the blood of Christ (Letters 61 and 163). Female writers had to face the classic anthropology of womanly weakness, a negative and limiting circumstance, which precisely because it was marked by sin, stood in need of redemption. However, for women who had a deep, direct relation with the Bible, and who meditated on the sacred texts, this very fragility became an opportunity to give value to the female experience and to "simple-heartedness" (which sometimes confounds the wise and the strong—see I Corinthians, 1:26-27) born of "love's intellect".

For instance, the Bible was used by the writer Christine de Pizan as a basis for moral and allegoric construction in *The Book of the City of Ladies* (1404), in which female presence is not measured by an arbitrary concept of gender, but by the exercise of virtues. Referring to Mary Magdalene, de Pizan insists on women's love.

> "Oh! What strong faith had those women who neither in life nor in death ever left the son of God, he who had been abandoned and deserted by all his apostles. It truly seems that God did not disdain the love of the women or that this was something weak. To the contrary, he himself endowed the heart of the blessed Mary Magdalene and the other women with the spark of this strong love that he approved so much." (Christine de Pizan, *The Book of the City of Ladies*, Book III, 2, translation from the Italian by Wendy Wheatley)

"The love that does not abandon" became the leitmotiv dear to the spiritual thinking of women who found in the devoted presence of Mary Magdalene the highest model to follow on the road to faith, seeing how she remained a firm, passionate disciple, contrary to the frightened, fleeing men.

As the poetess Vittoria Colonna, an authoritative exponent of pre-Reform Italian evangelism, writes to Cardinal Giovanni Morone, Mary Magdalene's "stout heart" allows the beloved disciple to meet the Risen One all alone, whom she had recognized neither with her eyes "of flesh" nor in the visibility of his appearances, but with the "interior eye of faith" that is born from love.

"Seeking him, he appeared to her resuscitated. Hearing his beloved voice address her with 'Mary,' she recognized with her heart the Teacher in another more divine awareness and more than ever she desired to find him and take comfort in him, but he showed her another road, namely to touch him, see him and serve him through his brethren, and he told her to go to them." (Vittoria Colonna, Epistola 164 in *Carteggio*, translation from the Italian by Wendy Wheatley)

Based on her direct reading of the Bible, Vittoria Colonna enriches the traditional hagiographic image that made Mary Magdalene the repentant par excellence, and turns her into a historical figure more faithful to the sources. The themes of ardent love are expanded with references to her privileged condition as a "beloved disciple" who

"deserved before everyone to see the glorious immortal giving clear testimony to the Lord, who to certify that she was his apostle, commanded her that she was the first heraldess of the awaited news and the wonderful mystery of his resurrection." (Vittoria Colonna, Epistola 170)

*

The favorite disciple, "made absolutely perfect and an erudite announcer of the divine Word," is rehabilitated in her complex symbology as a solitary repentant (see Colonna's *Rime spirituali*, "spiritual poems"), "as tearful as can be" (see the painting made for Colonna by Titian, mentioned in Epistola 42) and as a witness of the Truth. Regarding this, I refer to the cartoon drawn for Colonna by Michelangelo showing the *Noli me tangere* scene, later translated into painting by Pontormo. Those tears were not to be understood as the effect of the sins she had committed, rather as a sign of loving faith ("devotion") and adhesion to the divine will.

Mary Magdalene, who "with her stout heart and compassionate care remained alone" (*Rime spirituali*) was the symbol of women's steadfastness for being strong in love and open to hope, much to the contrary of the weak men who were stricken by fright and doubt. Her ardent, constant heart became the occasion for considerations of wider scope regarding the female gender. To Colonna, women merited more esteem.

> "The beautiful woman, in the aching grief
> of great longing, that chaser of all fears,
> by night, alone, defenseless, humble and pure,
> armed only with sharp ardent hope,
> she enters the tomb, and weeps and moans.
> She ignores the angels and heeds not her inner self,
> but falls securely at the feet of the Lord,
> for a heart aflame with love is afraid of nothing.
> And the strong men, elected to many graces,

huddled together in fear, saw the true light
merely as naked spirit and umbrage.
So if truth is not overshadowed by falsehood,
it behooves us to grant women the entire merit
of having hearts that kindle more constantly."
(Vittoria Colonna, *Rime spirituali*, translation from the
Italian by Wendy Wheatley)

In this manner, the apostle Magdalene constitutes a
model of promotion of the female role. Those happen to be
the same years in which the humanist Erasmus defended
learned and active women. For one of his *Colloquies* (1522)
he devised the female character of Magdalia, who in order
to criticize and ridicule an abbot who finds it misfitting for
a lady to pursue knowledge, defends the women's rights
that were forbidden by the Church at the time.

"If you [men] are not careful, the net result will be
that we'll preside in the theological schools, preach in
the churches, and wear your mitres," says the learned
lady in *The Abbot and Learned Woman* in *Colloquies* by
Erasmus of Rotterdam, 1522.[19]

The figure of Mary Magdalene is repeatedly referred to by
female Italian mystics and offers the opportunity to recuper-
ate a meaningful and captivating model in all its multitude of
facets. The conversion that calls for penance, the sorrowful
and faithful piety at the foot of the Cross, the impassioned
love that does not abandon the loved one, and above all the
announcement of the Lord's resurrection, all make Mary

Magdalene the emblem of a new feminine subjectivity. As a disciple and apostle, a repentant and evangelist, she represents the extraordinary fusion of active life and contemplative life.

Her faith is not nurtured by disquisitions, but born of experience, from the encounter with a person to love. The mystic Domenica Narducci, for example, dedicated one of her sermons to Mary Magdalene (Sermon II, 28 July 1516), whom she identifies as the forgiven sinner (Luke 7:36-50) in order to affirm that God favors faith that is born out of love and not social condition or superiority of gender. The female sinner is superior to Simon because unlike he who falsely considers himself to be righteous, she places her heart in the hands of Christ.

In the "mystic theater" present in the imaginative narrations by several visionaries including the Augustinian Veronica da Binasco, we see a broadening of the biblical text to give strength to several protagonists who have not been opportunely valorized. In Binasco's visions, the scenes reproduced have the connotation of a sacred representation where episodes taken from the canonical gospels are interwoven with ones taken from the apocryphal gospels and hagiographic legends. As already the case in all preceding tradition, she is identified erroneously with Martha's sister and the pardoned sinner. Here, Mary Magdalene, first a shameless woman, then a repentant disciple, is presented as a faithful friend, empathic to the suffering of the Virgin Mary. She is at the distraught mother's side; she is bidden to convince Jesus to not go toward his torture; she even desires the Nazarene dead in order to not see him suffer—the last two details are not found in the canonical gospels—and in the end she receives the revelation of the resurrection and is sent to the disciples. (Benedetta da Vimercate, *La virtuosa vita religiosa di suor Veronica*, 1501)

Pondering several excerpts from the gospels, Giovanna Maria della Croce (Bernardina Floriani), a Poor Clare, attempted to understand why the Lord chose Mary Magdalene, "a woman and of the weaker sex," and established her as "a preacheress and ambassadress of the apostles, making them receive from her the good news of his glorious resurrection" (Speech for Sunday the 17th after Pentecost, 1634). The Magdalene's fervent faith led to an ardent love for Christ, who conceded her "the privilege of being made secretary of God and aware of the divine mysteries" (ibidem).

A different slant is found in the interpretation given by the proto-feminist nun Arcangela Tarabotti, who refers to the figure of Mary Magdalene in order to defend women from the accusation of being of a different nature and inferior compared to men. In her last writing, *Che le donne siano della specie degli uomini* ("That women are of the same species as men", 1651), the Benedictine nun gives an answer to a misogynistic treatise by Orazio Plata. Tarabotti refutes his affirmation that

"Christ first appeared to women for no other reason than his resurrection would thus be published to the world immediately and as rapidly as possible. Since women are garrulous, the whole city immediately learns what they know. It is the case that a woman may testify according neither to divine nor to human law. And therefore Christ could not have them as witnesses to his resurrection, since their testimony is invalid." (*Disputatio Nova Contra Mulieres/A New Argument Against Women*, 1595)[20]

In her opposition to Orazio Plata, Arcangela Tarabotti underlines Christ's choice as given by his gratitude for having received help and compassion from "womanly piety and goodness." Contrary to the men who had betrayed and abandoned him, the women took care of him. For this, "he wanted to elect them as the genuine witnesses of his resurrection" and appeared "to his very beloved apostle" (*Che le donne*).

Mary Magdalene was the favorite saint of many religious Catholic women, from Teresa of Ávila to Therese of Lisieux, and of mystics who even chose her name in a sort of hagiographic imitation. Examples are Mary Magdalene de' Pazzi (christened Caterina) and Mary Magdalene Martinengo (christened Margherita). Also women linked to the Protestant Reformation took on the model represented by Mary Magdalene. Although the Protestant Reformation rested on the centrality of the Bible and the recognition of universal priesthood, it neither changed the condition of women immediately nor did it easily surpass preconceived anthropological notions and cultural models. The women who appealed for a different and more significant consideration within the Church did not have an easy time. The example given by Mary Magdalene and the other female disciples has served to ask for dignity and roles. Margaret Fell, one of the founders of the Quaker movement, championed women and fought for their right to preach.

"What had become of the redemption of the whole body of mankind, if they had not cause to believe the message that the Lord Jesus sent by these women [Mary Magdalene, Mary the mother of James, etcetera] of and concerning his resurrection? And if these women had not thus, out of their tenderness, and bowels of love, who had received mercy and grace and forgiveness of sins, and virtue, and healing from him? Which many men also had received the like, if the hearts of the women had not been so united and knit unto him in love, that they could not depart as the men did?" (Margaret Fell, *Women's Speaking Justified*, 1666)

The African American Jarena Lee was another preacheress who had to defend her pastoral role, as it was contested within the Methodist Episcopal Church in the early 19th century.

"If the man may preach, because the Saviour died for him, why not the woman, seeing he died for her also? [. . .] Did not Mary *first* preach the risen Saviour, and is not the doctrine of the resurrection the very climax of Christianity? [. . .] Then did not Mary, a woman, preach the gospel? For she preached the resurrection of the crucified Son of God." (Jarena Lee, *Religious Experience and Journal of Mrs. Jarina Lee, giving an account of her call to preach the gospel,* 1849)

Returning to modern times, Mary Magdalene was a reference model for the Order of Sorority founded by Ivana Ceresa. In her eyes, the Risen One called Mary Magdalene to divulge throughout the world previously unknown relations of sisterhood and brotherhood. In her book *L'utopia e la conserva* (2011), Ceresa states that "Mary of Magdala is the highest authorization for a Christian woman to feel involved in the proclamation of the Gospel. And for a woman, this is no trifle—namely, knowing that there is a female authority."

Critical humanism and Protestant controversies

Starting with the comparative study *Annotations on the New Testament* (1444) by Lorenzo Valla, published in 1505 by Erasmus, secular thought began taking its first progressive steps away from the apologetic and dogmatic use of sacred texts. The philological approach, historical sensibility and new philosophical premises—put into place by Renaissance humanism and taken up by the Enlightenment—represented a turning-point in the field of bible studies and marked in this sense a slow and intricate path to independence from the ecclesiastic authorities, opening the road to the historical and critical method of the 19th century. In this first period, doubts began to arise about the fusion of the figures connected to Mary Magdalene and the reliability of the legends about her. With his bible studies, the humanist and theologian Jacques Lefèvre d'Étaples (*De Maria Magdalena et triduo Christi disceptatio*, 1517-1518, and *De tribus et unica Magdalena*, 1519) calls into question the identification of the three Marys, but when his writings were condemned in 1525 he was forced into exile and shifted closer in thought to the ideas of the Reformation. The Lutheran crisis was about to break loose. Among Protestant theologians, there was an increasing tendency, albeit not without heated debate, to distinguish the female figures grouped under the one name, and to refuse unitary hypotheses. In addition, the hagiographic traditions were condemned for being considered legendary; the cults for the saints were reputed papistical superstitions. Ulrich Zwingli wanted the cult of Mary Magdalene abolished; John Calvin derided her legend.

Yet within the Reformation, the Lutherans did not entirely cancel the cult of the saints. They rejected their role as intercessors and patrons in favor of the model of the witnesses of the Gospel, and even several images were tolerated if they were capable of fostering faith and pointing it in the direction of the reformed truths. For instance, Mary Magdalene was taken up again by the German reformer Hermann Bonnus as an example of a believer touched by mercy (*Farrago praecipuorum exemplorum*, 1539) and in Protestant liturgy she was remembered as a beneficiary of the clemency of God. Mary Magdalene earned salvation in virtue of the love and faith bestowed upon her by God out of mercy, therefore she is functional to the diffusion of the principle of justification out of faith. This didactic scheme is illustrated by a painter at the court of Frederick of Saxony, named Lucas Cranach the Elder. He was the creator of the new Protestant iconography. In two paintings he revisits the figure of the disciple in a Christocentric key (*Christ and Mary Magdalene*, around 1520) as well as in the evangelical forms of an elegant and refined myrrh-bearer (*Mary Magdalene*, 1525), freeing her from every hint of idolatry.

In his painting *Christ and Saint Mary Magdalene at the Tomb* (1638), Rembrandt van Rijn looks to the episode in the Gospel of John that allows him to underline the personal meditation and spiritual intimacy that originate in the encounter with Christ.

Emblem of the Counter-Reformation

Paradoxically, while in the Reformation Mary Magdalene is taken as a symbol of the benevolent grace of God, the Counter-Reformation makes her a model of repentance, and therefore an encouragement to the practice of frequent confession, denied by Protestantism. The merits earned by the saint's acts of mortification are counterposed by the Catholic Church to Martin Luther's "justification by faith alone" doctrine.

In artistic representations found in the Catholic area, the "sinner saint" takes on not only the traits of the converted prostitute, but also those of the woman intent on a life of ascesis and contemplation. This is why her portraits were so requested by courtesans wishing for divine protection, by worshippers seeking examples of humble and internal spirituality, and by many aristocratic women pleased to have themselves painted in the devout manner of Mary Magdalene. When it underlines the qualities of sin, this iconography accentuates the erotic image of a beautiful and seductive body. See the *Penitent Mary Magdalene* by Titian, with its evident sensuality emphasized by long blond hair ("Titian hair") that barely covers the nudity of her body.

At the same time, the art made under the Counter-Reformation shows the themes of tears and repentance, portraying the saint in prayer, withdrawn in thought by an inner pain, with a skull, candle or mirror by her side as symbols of vanity and the fragility of the human condition. See the two portraits of the Penitent Magdalene (1630 and 1640) by Georges de la Tour, which include both elements of meditation (books) and symbols of life's fugacity (skull, lamp, mirror, abandoned jewelry). Conversion and penitence can be a departure point for a new life.

Such imagery—hung on the walls of chapels, convents and monasteries, seen in the paintings commissioned by the aristocracy, or in tablets made for use at home—interacts constantly with the meditational writings by spiritual directors and with the words of preachers, contributing to the creation of devotions, the implementation of religious practices and the elaboration of an individual and collective spirituality focused on the themes of sin and redemption.

The countless literary compositions dedicated to Mary Magdalene in the baroque era became tools for moral edification. They revisit the steps of conversion of the "beautiful woman," from the attachment to worldly goods to their renouncement, emphasizing the ambivalence present in her figure: the sacred and the profane, the spiritual and the carnal. Among the many examples that can be made testifying to this are: the short poem *Le Lagrime di M. Maddalena* by Erasmo da Valvasone (1586); the verses by Giovan Battista Marino (1602); the novel *Maria Maddalena peccatrice e convertita* by Anton Giulio Brignole Sale (1636), the drama *La Maddalena lasciva e penitente* by Giovan Battista Andreini (1652), and the burlesque poem *La Magdaléide* by Pierre de Saint-Louis (1668). All are mirrors of the disquieted spirit of the times. In these works, Mary Magdalene, "the beloved lover of Christ" (Giovan Battista Marino, *Galeria*, 1619), is the protagonist of a profound metamorphosis that exalts the life of luxury and pleasures she led before her conversion.

"Once she had opened wide to Bacchus and Venus, she became a school of impure luxuries, where a delicious plague of Arabic odors mixed in the air with stench wafting from rude mouths. The labors of Persian needles flourished in fine tapestries and the torment of hammers wielded to work gold into objects shimmered, making Magdalene appear rich in everything except the soul." (Anton Giulio Brignole Sale, *Maria Maddalena peccatrice e convertita*, 1636, translation from the Italian by Wendy Wheatley)

La Conversione della Maddalena (around 1658), a painting

by Guido Cagnacci, makes explicit this contrast between sacred and profane through the portrayal of her nude and seductive body sensually reclining, encircled by the sumptuous gown and rich jewelry she has removed. In the background we see the fight of a good angel (virtue) driving away the Devil (vice) and in the foreground Martha exhorts her to leave her sinful life.

The artistic, pictorial and literary works are linked to sermons, especially the ones prepared for the Lenten period, which were best suited to arouse deep feeling and compunction. See the intense pages of sentimental theology dedicated to her by the Dominican preacher Louis Chardon in his mystical *The Cross of Jesus* (1647); the *Sermons* of Francis de Sales (1567-1622); the *Quaresimale* (1879) by the Jesuit preacher Paolo Segneri; *La Maddalena penitente* (1690) by the Dominican preacher Giovanni Maria Muti; and the *Prediche quaresimali postume* (1702) by the Jesuit Giacomo Lubrano.

In modern times, institutes that took care of street women were established under the name of Mary Magdalene. In 1833, Giulia di Barolo founded the Sorelle Penitenti di Santa Maria Maddalena (now Figlie di Gesù Buon Pastore) with the aim of reinserting prostitutes into society by giving them an education and teaching them a trade.

In the 19th century, consideration of Mary Magdalene was tinged with the typical colors of the times' romantic spirit.

In his essay *The Life of Jesus* (1795), the young philosopher Hegel meditates on the essence of Christianity as a vision of the world established on the sentiment of love, and lauds Mary Magdalene's "beautiful soul permeated by sacrifice, trust and love," saying that she was not understood by the "too cold heart" of the disciples used to respecting the abstract law and intellectual reasoning. The beauty that sprang from the gesture of love expressed by the "sinner" (as the saint was still perceived in the 19th century) is interpreted not only as a fundamental element for the fulfillment of a harmonious human being made of sentiment and intellect, but also as the incarnation of the Eternal Feminine, a definition of mysterious resonance that is made explicit in the final scene of Goethe's play *Faust* (1808). At the end of the work, the poet takes on the theme of the redemption, making a Mater Gloriosa ("queen and ruler of the world") appear in the company of a procession of three women—Magna Peccatrix (Mary Magdalene), Mulier Samaritana (the woman at the well) and Maria Aegyptiaca (Mary of Egypt). The "female penitents" express the creative force that moves the universe, the feminine principle of love, salvation. "Woman, eternal, beckons us on," is the last phrase of the epic spoken by the Mystic Choir: the human soul, mystery of the world, yearns for the spiritual.

In this period, however, the figure of Mary Magdalene tied to the theme of "redemptive love" is strongly called into question by the establishment of historical and exegetical studies of the sacred scripture. [21]

The considerations of the philologist and biblical scholar Ernest Renan were without scruple. In *Life of Jesus* (1863) he examines the gospels critically, underlining the elements of enthusiasm and passion felt by the women who love Jesus.

> "Three or four devoted Galilean women always accompanied the young Master, and disputed among themselves the pleasure of listening to him and tending him in turn." (Chapter 9)[22]

According to Renan, however, such sentiment did not turn out to be advantageous for the credibility of Christianity, seeing that faith in the resurrection rests on Mary Magdalene, a woman of "strong imagination" (Chapter 27). Her love was what created the myth of Christianity, and this made Renan exclaim cynically, "Divine power of love [. . .] in which the passion of one possessed gave to the world a resuscitated God!" (Chapter 26).

The lover, the companion, the bride of Jesus

Although in 1912 the theologian Garrigou-Lagrange had confuted in a definitive way the identification of the three Marys, closing the controversy opened in the 16th century by Jacques Lefèvre d'Étaples, the literature and cinematography of the 20th century reinvigorated the distorted image of Mary Magdalene, and—mystical and devotional aspects aside—they were directed at more realistic and provocatory meanings. See the unusual point of view held by Marguerite Yourcenar in the lyrical prose of *Mary Magdalene* (part of her book *Fires* published in 1936). Willfully unfaithful to the historical record, but interested in the meaning of total and unhappy love, the writer has Mary Magdalene appear, through the literary fiction of the confession, as a woman betrayed and disappointed by unrequited love. She was abandoned—first by John the apostle, her promised husband who flees on the night of the wedding to follow the voice of God (*The Golden Legend*, XCII, 182–187); then by men to whom she had given herself for a love that she never really enjoyed; and lastly by Jesus, who in order to fulfill his mission as a savior, sacrificed his life, leaving her alone in despair in front of the empty tomb. It was above all her love for Christ, her impossible lover, that brings her pain. The awareness of an inescapable defeat delivers her to unhappiness.

"So as not to ruin his career as Saviour, I consented to see him die as a mistress consents to the rich marriage of the man she loves." (Yourcenar, *Fires*)[23]

There is nothing left for her to do but inveigh against a cruel God who conceded her "only a crumb of the infinite love," condemning her to misery forever. "God saved me neither from death nor from harm nor from crime, since it's through these things that one is saved. He saved me from happiness."

The Portuguese novelist José Saramago also turned his hand to describing the figure of Mary Magdalene. In *The Gospel According to Jesus Christ* (1991) he describes the relationship between Jesus and the sinner as the encounter between two types of solitude: that of a young man lacking in affection and recognition, and that of a prostitute longing to receive attention in order to regain her dignity as a woman. Seeking security and protection, she passionately falls in love with Jesus and leaves her profession as a prostitute to become his lover.

> "After this conversation, Mary served Jesus food, and he did not have to tell her, 'Sit with me,' for since their first day together behind locked doors this man and this woman have divided and multiplied between them feelings, gestures, spaces, and sensations without paying much attention to the rules and laws." (José Saramago, *The Gospel According to Jesus Christ*)[24]

Receiving from Jesus the tenderness and attention she needs, Mary Magdalene accompanies her cherished man to the end. She is the only one to remain close to him at the hour of trial, and suffered atrociously for the death of her loved one, in contrast to Mary the mother, who remains distant. Both Saramago and Yourcenar emphasize the tragic figure of the Magdalene, marked by the irreconcilability of sacred love and profane love, by the incomprehension of a God of love who paradoxically is unable to love a woman to the fullest.

Warm sensuality is found in the poetry by Alda Merini, who writes of the beauty of Mary Magdalene at first as "a throw-away container" (*un vuoto a perdere*) sullied by kisses from men who never understood her, and finally as a woman understood by Jesus who speaks to her and restores her dignity. "I was so intact, Lord, under your gaze, that you saw and chose me as the first discipless." Although Jesus healed "the wounds of her spirit," Magdalene was unable to reciprocate.

"The salt of my lips will heal / your many wounds: / you have scraped your feet, Jesus, / let me medicate them with my hair, / you will feel in my hair the freshness of linen / and your lesions will close. / In truth, Jesus, / I do not know who informed me of your destiny, / but I love you and know everything about you, / like any woman / who loves her own husband." (Alda Merini, *Maria Maddalena* in *Cantico dei Vangeli*, 2006, translated from the Italian by Wendy Wheatley)

As we mention in Chapter 1, the question of the carnal love between Jesus and the Magdalene is touched upon in the two literary texts *The Last Temptation of Christ* (1951) by Nikos Kazantzakis and *The Da Vinci Code* (2003) by Dan Brown, both of which offered the material for two successful movies—the former directed by Martin Scorsese in 1988 and the latter by Ron Howard in 2006.

The Last Temptation deals with the subject of the sexual desire and inner turmoil of a man continuously torn between his attraction for a woman, the Magdalene, and the will to refuse her. Jesus succeeds in resisting seduction in the name of God, but on the Cross, close to death, his wish for progeny re-emerges and he dreams of an earthly life with a wife and children (first with Mary Magdalene; then upon her death, with Martha). Only the thought of the good of humanity in need of salvation helps Jesus accomplish his sacrifice and reject the last temptation.

Here too, the woman is seen as an enticement and not as a positive life opportunity, confirming the archetype of feminine erotic seduction that is redeemed to the extent in which she transcends her own sensuality either by travelling a road of penitence and atonement, or by excising it for a higher ideal.

In *The Da Vinci Code*, on the other hand, Mary Magdalene is the conscious wife of Jesus, his favorite disciple, and the mother of a girl named Sarah. Persecuted by the misogynistic Church, she flees to Gaul, bringing with her the daughter she had with Jesus and from whom would descend the Merovingian dynasty. "A woman who carried with her a secret so powerful that, if revealed, it threatened to devastate the very foundation of Christianity!" The secret—that Sarah was the material continuation of the "sacred" blood, from which would derive the Holy Grail— would later arrive at the Knights Templar.

"Mary Magdalene was the Holy Vessel. She was the chalice that bore the royal bloodline of Jesus Christ. She was the womb that bore the lineage, and the vine from which the sacred fruit sprang forth!" (Dan Brown)[25]

No biblical or historical source validates such theses sustained by the American novelist, who deftly mixes legends, oddities and the collective imagination to the backdrop of an esoteric and adventurous plot. Above all, Brown was able to emphasize the conflict present in the Gnostic gospels between the superior charisma of the Magdalene, who symbolizes knowledge and spiritual communion, and the misogynistic authority of Peter, who represents the institution, thereby corroborating the compelling hypothesis of a womankind that was rejected and marginalized by the Church. By constructing the fortunate theory of Mary Magdalene as the "bride" of Jesus, the writer has stirred up questions that were too often left unanswered, favoring the reopening of studies on the weight of the sexual taboo within religious structures (which also applies to Jesus from Nazareth) and on the role of women in the Church.

Especially this latter branch of exploration has shifted attention to Mary Magdalene. She is no longer seen as one of many characters in evangelical history, but as an actual protagonist. See the television movie *Maria Maddalena* (2000) by the Italian director Raffaele Mertes, where however the saint is still presented in the cliché of the converted prostitute, and the one by the Australian television director Garth Davis, *Mary Magdalene* (2018), which goes against the literary and cinematographic stereotypes to restitute her true identity as a disciple. Freeing her from all sexual ambiguity, Davis's Magdalene finds in her encounter with Jesus a spiritual understanding that allows her to travel her path independently from familial structures, sharing with him the message of liberation and salvation. It is clear that by proposing this reading of the evangelical figure, the director is indebted to studies that female theologians have been conducting in their research into women for over 40 years.

Championess of women in the Church

After the Second Vatican Council (1962–1965), the Catholic Theological Faculties were opened to the laity, resulting in a constant and growing commitment by women. By acquiring the tools of scientific research, they have been able to pose new questions of the theological disciplines, revitalizing them from the inside. Thanks above all to the American and German schools, feminist hermeneutic viewpoints have implemented the "hermeneutics of suspicion" (as defined by Elisabeth Schüssler Fiorenza in her book *In Memory of Her: A Feminist Theological Reconstruction of Christian Origins*, 1983), which casts a shadow on the texts in which the presence of women is ignored or willfully eliminated. For the German theologian Fiorenza, it is important to not trust biblical passages that obey patriarchal criteria and, moreover, to search in them the not entirely erased traces of significant roles played by women. In order to do this, it is necessary to find ways to break the silence of the texts, thoroughly broadening the research field. The figure of Mary Magdalene is precisely an example of this, downplayed by the evangelist Luke, who minimizes her role as the first witness in the gospel as well as in the Acts of the Apostles. Comparison of the other canonical gospels with the Gnostic gospels and coeval literature has shown how the passage from apostle to prostitute has been functional to the patriarchal system that nipped in the bud the possibility of guiding roles of women in the Church. In this sense, for feminist theology it appears indispensable to render justice to the historical figure of Mary Magdalene and the women who were not marginal in the formation process of Christianity.

In the last 30 years, conferences, research and publications dedicated to her have blossomed all over the Christian world. These have offered new indications for research and interesting interpretative perspectives. Especially the rediscovery of her apostolate has reopened the discussion about Jesus's discipleship and the role of women. Mary Magdalene has become the champion of a Church reform that places the evangelical message and the assertion of a "discipleship of equals" at its center, in order to valorize the role of every baptized person by recognizing women's capacity to be authoritative guides.

This is the direction in which the work by the theologian and painter Dina Cormick leads. Through the iconographic re-elaboration of female biblical figures, she calls for a different position for women in the Church. Her

1992 dissertation for the University of South Africa, "The Visual Portrayal of Mary Magdalene: A Case Study in Feminist Ethical Issues," gave life to a series of didactic images. Based mostly on the Gnostic texts, they underline Mary Magdalene's leading role among the disciples, turning her into an archetype of liberation for Christian women.

The evangelizing woman in the Church of Pope Francis

Pope Francis has shown himself to be particularly sensitive to questions related to giving value to the role of women within the ecclesiastical community. On 3 June 2016, by his express wish, the celebration of Saint Mary Magdalene (held on 22 July) was elevated and inscribed in the General Roman Calendar with the rank of Feast, placing the celebration on the same level as those dedicated to the other apostles. Seeing she is the Apostle of the Apostles, "who so loved Christ and was so greatly loved by Christ," as Rabanus Maurus affirms, she was the first to see the risen Christ and the first to announce it to the apostles. By doing this, the pope has wanted to underline the importance of the first witness of the resurrection by giving emphasis to her role as an evangelizer and "the special mission of this woman, she who is an example and model for all women in the Church." (Decree of the Congregation for Divine Worship and the Discipline of the Sacraments, 3 June 2016)

The decree gives the feast a new preface, the solemn

prayer to recite during the first part of the Canon. In it, the Magdalene and her presence in the life of Jesus are praised:

Preface of the Apostle of the Apostles

"It is truly right and just, our duty and our salvation, always and everywhere to give you thanks, Lord, holy Father, almighty and eternal God, whose mercy is no less than His power, to preach the Gospel to everyone, through Christ, our Lord. In the garden He appeared to Mary Magdalene, who loved him in life, who witnessed his death on the cross, who sought him as he lay in the tomb, who was the first to adore him when he rose from the dead, and whose apostolic duty was honored by the apostles, so that the good news of life might reach the ends of the earth. And so Lord, with all the Angels and Saints, we, too, give you thanks, as in exultation we acclaim: Holy, holy, holy Lord, God of power and might."

CHAPTER 6
ICONOGRAPHIC IMAGES AND SYMBOLS

To enclose Mary Magdalene only in the historical dimension leads to a loss of richness, seeing how her hagiographic figure has been constructed over centuries as a multiform and complex personality. As a highly popular saint, Mary Magdalene has become an archetype, having grouped together three discrete female identities that allowed her to condense within her several important stereotypes of womanhood, and by consequence be considered a model for the many people who recognize themselves in her.

In relation to the episodes of her life that were attributed to her, she has been elected the patron of several categories of people: perfumers (for her presence at the tomb with a jar of ointment—"faithful perfumeress" as Rabanus Maurus describes her in *The Life of Saint Mary Magdalene and of Her Sister Saint Martha*, Chapter 26); hairdressers (thanks to the flowing hair with which she dries Jesus's wet feet); gardeners (for the place where she encounters the risen Christ); and sinners (for her life before conversion, redeemed by penitence).

The iconographic repertory that regards her is incredibly vast, ranging from images with a sensual character—and here she appears young, seductive, transgressive and with long, untied hair—to images with a more spiritual meaning—and here we see a pensive, penitent and meditative person. Artists depict her at the foot of the Cross or in conversation with the risen Christ; in the role of the repentant and forgiven prostitute; or as a disciple listening to the words of the Teacher from Galilee. Over time, each era has privileged some element, though variations were few. Each artist has projected onto her their own ideal of a woman, either in harmony or in discord with the abundant theological and devotional tradition. Sometimes the stylistic elements are used in an unoriginal manner; other times they tap intricate texts where the sober evangelical verses were blended with erroneous interpretations due either to false identifications with Martha's sister and with the repentant prostitute, or hagiographic legends such as the tale of Saint Mary of Egypt and the imaginary reconstruction of *The Golden Legend*.

The Florentine painting *Mary Magdalene with Eight Scenes from her Life* is precious proof of the cult of the Magdalene and the mixing of evangelical stories and popular tales. Around a large hieratic picture of the saint are illustrated eight events linked to her legendary existence: *Resurrection of Lazarus*; *Mary Magdalene Anointing Christ's Feet*; *Noli Me Tangere*; *Mary Magdalene Preaching in France*; *An Angel Feeding Mary Magdalene in the Desert*; *Mary Magdalene Borne to Heaven by Angels*; *Mary Magdalene's Last Communion*; and *Funeral of Mary Magdalene*.

After these medieval cycles, frequently found in France and Italy, came an increasing number of single scenes, starting in the 16th century in monasteries and churches of the mendicant and penitent orders. Often these pictures are figurative syntheses of complex elements. Below is my attempt to schematize the most recurrent iconographic motifs with the aim of ending the misunderstandings by disentangling the delicate questions related to the identification of Mary Magdalene and by pointing out the source from which the different artists took inspiration.

These are just a few examples of the many artists inspired by the saint.

The biblical models

The myrrh-bearer. Together with several women, Mary Magdalene goes to the tomb on Easter morning to sprinkle Jesus's body with aromatic perfume.

> "On the first day of the week, at the first sign of dawn, they went to the tomb with the spices they had prepared. [. . .] The women were Mary of Magdala, Joanna, and Mary the mother of James." (Luke 24:1 and 10)

The jar of perfume is iconographically her main element of recognizability. It connects not only to the scented oil poured on Jesus's feet (Luke 7:38) and the ointment needed to prepare his body for burial, but also represents the welcoming and safekeeping of the message of salvation. Paul the Apostle was defined a "chosen instrument" (vessel) in which is deposited the mission of announcing

Christ's name to all peoples (Acts of the Apostles 9:15) and Paul uses this symbolism to indicate the Christian condition: a fragile "pot" in the hands of God (Romans 9:20). Therefore, the believer is defined *vas Christi* in Christian epigraphy.

Another distinctive element to recognize Mary Magdalene in the group of women bringing the aromatics is the long, untied hair, often blond, which alludes to her preceding condition of prostitute, assigned to her mistakenly by tradition and taken up slavishly by artists, without regard for the historical anachronism when they portray her with the symbols of sin even after her conversion.

Often the saint is represented together with other women, for instance by Annibale Carracci in *The Pious Women at Christ's Tomb* (around 1600), where her figure stands out for the loose blonde hair without a head covering. Other times, she is seen alone with her jar of perfume, as in Piero della Francesca, who depicts her in a proud posture with a particularly shiny ampulla in her hand. Jan Gossaert shows her as a splendid lady, sitting opulently dressed as she clasps a closed urn. Lucas Cranach the Elder portrays her as an elegant blond noblewoman standing in front of a background of lush greenery. Carlo Dolci paints the Magdalene as a dreamy, mystical girl, arms crossed over her chest, clutching the jar of unguent in one hand.

Christ's Passion. The dramatic setting of a meagerly narrated scene in the gospels—"Near the cross of Jesus stood his mother and his mother's sister, Mary the wife of Clopas, and Mary of Magdala." (John 19:25)—allowed artists to express themselves with freedom, representing Mary Magdalene in different poses. Sometimes she's in a group: in the sculpture by Giovanni di Rigino, *Deposition of Christ in the Tomb* (1380), she is seen with Joseph of Arimathea, John, the Virgin Mary and Nicodemus. Other times she is desperate but alone: see *Crocifisso con la Maddalena* (around 1500) by Luca Signorelli. In the *Deposition from the Cross* by Rosso Fiorentino (1521) she is shown with other women and the Madonna, whose knees she embraces. In a *Crucifixion* from around 1515 by Matthias Grünewald, as well as in *The Descent from the Cross* by Pieter Paul Rubens (around 1612), she is portrayed with the Madonna and the disciple John.

Often the mother's pained decorum is counterposed to the Magdalene's agitated manner. See for instance the unfinished work *Pietà* (1576) by Titian, where she advances distraughtly, shouting in grief over the death of Jesus, who lies recumbent in Mary's arms. The themes of Lamentation (in work by Niccolò dell'Arca and by Guido Mazzoni) and Deposition are not present in the gospels but widely represented throughout the centuries in artwork that emphasizes the anguished scene of desperation around the lifeless body of Jesus. This iconographic tradition, from which Caravaggio distanced himself by painting Mary Magdalene with her head bowed in subdued suffering in *The Entombment of Christ* (around 1604), was taken up again in the 19th century with more drama (see *The Lamentations of Mary Magdalene on the Body of Christ* by Arnold Böcklin, 1867), intensity and vibrancy (*The Three Marys at the Foot of the Cross* by Gaetano Previati, 1891).

And in the 20th century, the interpretation of Mary Magdalene became entirely human. She became a victim of the world's violence and pain. Her suffering became a universal symbol of piety and compassion. Examples of this are the *Crucifixion* painting (1941) by Renato Guttuso in which a naked Magdalene desperately clutches at the bloodless body of Christ in a setting that recalls the tragedy of war; *Figure Study II* (1946) by Francis Bacon, who expresses the sense of despair with an anguished scream exiting the woman's enlarged, gaping mouth; and the bronze relief *Morte del partigiano* (1960) by Giacomo Manzù, where Jesus is portrayed as a modern-day political martyr looked upon with compassion by the woman.

Noli me tangere. The expression *Noli me tangere* ("Do not wish to touch me") evokes Mary Magdalene's encounter with the risen Christ by the empty tomb. It is usually interpreted as Christ's refusal to be touched, or more correctly, to be held back, seeing he must ascend to the Father (John 20:16-17).

The themes of searching for the Beloved one, being called by name, the desire to cling to Jesus out of loving instinct, and the painful detachment are all subjects that are represented diversely by each artist according to which element of the encounter they wish to underline. This episode is widely represented in the history of art, and has offered the occasion to plastically express the physicality of the characters in the desired but negated contact of their bodies.

And so there are different pictorial examples ranging

from the sobriety and simplicity of paintings by Giotto and
Beato Angelico—in which the two are kept at a benevolent
distance from each other—to the more tragic work by
Titian, where Jesus shifts away his hips and gracefully
moves his mantle just out of reach of Mary Magdalene,
whose expression is incredulous and happily surprised.
Then there is Correggio's representation that emphasizes
the expressivity of the two protagonists' psychological
reactions. Christ raises one hand on the right, pointing
upward, and with the other hand he retains distance from
a dismayed Mary Magdalene, who kneels on the ground to
the left, wanting to embrace him. Rembrandt opts for a
somber setting where the tension between presence and
absence creates a contemplative atmosphere of meditation
on life and death. The classically inspired version of *Noli
me tangere* by Nicolas Poussin exalts the monumentality of
the characters, who almost touch each other in an imaginary embrace. Laurent de la Hyre paints Christ reaching
toward Mary Magdalene's brow to shield her eyes from seeing him.

The *Noli me tangere* theme refers to the physical and
spiritual dimension of corporeal contact, which is at once
union and separation, desire and loss, warm affection and
distance. The portrayal of the play of hands—those of
Christ and those of the Magdalene—shows how they come
close but do not touch, like a dialogue of profound and
silent love that feels the presence yet acknowledges the
absence at the same time.

In his book *Noli Me Tangere* (originally published in
French in 2003), the French philosopher Jean-Luc Nancy

writes: "This is why painters have been able to discern in it not the ecstatic vision of a miracle but a delicate intrigue that takes shape between the visible and the invisible, each of the two calling and repelling the other, each almost touching the other, then distancing themselves."[26]

A composite of symbols

Prostitute. We have seen how the gesture of anointment by an anonymous prostitute (Luke) or by Mary of Bethany (John) has been wrongly attributed to Mary Magdalene, who for centuries has been considered the sinner full of love that Jesus takes in. Sometimes the gesture is attributed to Martha's sister accomplishing a prophetic gesture.

> "A woman came in, who had a bad name in the town. She had heard he was dining with the Pharisee and had brought with her an alabaster jar of ointment. She waited behind him at his feet, weeping, and her tears fell on his feet, and she wiped them away with her hair; then she covered his feet with kisses and anointed them with the ointment." (Luke 7:37-38)

Representations of this evangelical theme often show iconographic variations. The anointing at Bethany (Luke 7:36-50 and John 12:1-8) is depicted more frequently than the version in which the anonymous sinner pours oil on Jesus's head (Mark 14:3-9 and Matthew 26:6-13). Many times, Mary Magdalene is portrayed alone in pictures that make explicit her character of provocative sensuality, sometimes painting her naked (see Titian), other times showing her in comely, elegant poses (see Artemisia Gentileschi). The interpretation given by Dante Gabriel Rossetti in his pen drawing *Mary Magdalene at the Door of Simon the Pharisee* (1858) is original and impactful. He accentuates her ambiguity, portraying her as sensual yet spiritual even before her encounter with Jesus.

Penitent. The iconographic renderings depicting Mary Magdalene as repentant for her sins are diverse.

> "Then he said to her, 'Your sins are forgiven.' [. . .] 'Your faith has saved you; go in peace.'" (Luke 7:48-50)

As we have seen, Titian puts on display the sensuality of her nude body—indicating the absence from earthly attachments—covered only by her loosely flowing hair. El Greco presents her ready to undress from her precious clothing, with a skull close by, the bible in hand, and her eyes turned up toward the divine light. Georges de la Tour depicts her absorbed in meditation on the vanity of worldly things, facing a mirror and a melting candle, which symbolizes the brevity of life. In this way, the subject of the penitence is connected to both the Vanitas theme that was very present in ascetic spirituality, and the Melancholia theme first favored by philosophical thought and back in vogue during humanism. The pained nostalgia for Jesus's absence is recognized in the painting *Melancholy* (around 1620) by Domenico Fetti, which has a clear connection to the engraving *Melencolia I* (1514) by Albrecht Dürer and communicates somber reflection on the human condition. Hendrick ter Brugghen, with *Melancolia* or *Mary Magdalene* (1627-1628) accentuates the sadness of the woman's face, surrounded by mysterious obscurity, contemplating human mortality. Another tone is given by the intense, sensual interpretation by Artemisia Gentileschi titled *Mary Magdalene as Melancholy* (around 1621-1625), where she is languidly slouched in a chair, absorbed in her memories.

When he painted *Penitent Magdalene* in 1595, Caravaggio freed the saint from the devotional interpretations of traditional Catholic iconography by portraying her as an everyday girl, alone, seated on a low chair with her hair untied, head bowed and hands on her lap. Her expression is forlorn and a tear runs down one cheek from her left eye. Jewelry thrown on the floor alludes to her break with her former life. The solitude of the woman flooded with light suggests a direct conciliation with God by means of sincere regret.

The same solitude is seen in the 18th century with Giacomo Ceruti, who accentuates the pietistic and penitential aspect of a weeping Magdalene; with Giuseppe Maria Crespi, who represents her in the grotto sensually clasping a crucifix; and with Antonio Canova, who renders in marble the woman's sensual beauty through composed, controlled sorrow. In times closer to ours, Giovanni Costetti portrays her isolated, bent and miserable with long hair hiding her face.

The image of Magdalene meditating in the grotto is

often modelled on the representation of Saint Jerome, including the symbols of skull and book, or else it shows clear inspiration from the iconography of Mary of Egypt, the courtesan from Alexandria who after conversion decides to retreat to the desert in penitence, covered only by her long hair. The iconographic element that distinguishes Mary of Egypt from Mary Magdalene is three loaves of bread instead of the jar. According to legend, Maria Aegyptiaca, as she is also known, miraculously survived in the desert on the three loaves she bought before undertaking her journey into the desert. Jusepe de Ribera, for instance, paints Mary of Egypt in a famous portrait from 1641 as an emaciated woman, no longer young, her nudity covered by sackcloth, with a skull and three loaves of bread. In the same period, Ribera painted a penitent Magdalene draped with her own hair, in contemplative prayer in front of a cross leaning on a skull, with a jar by her side. They are two mirror images in which the stories of the two saints connect and blend together.

Contemplative. The contemplative Mary Magdalene was born from the conflation of her and Mary of Bethany, the sister of Martha.

> "In the course of their journey he came to a village, and a woman named Martha welcomed him into her house. She had a sister called Mary, who sat down at the Lord's feet and listened to him speaking. Now Martha who was distracted with all the serving said, 'Lord, do you not care that my sister is leaving me to do

the serving all by myself? Please tell her to help me.' But the Lord answered: 'Martha, Martha,' he said 'you worry and fret about so many things, and yet few are needed, indeed only one. It is Mary who has chosen the better part; it is not to be taken from her.'" (Luke 10:38-42)

By taking up this episode from the gospel according to Luke—where the two sisters welcome Jesus into their house as one of them (Mary) starts listening to the Master and the other one (Martha) occupies herself with serving him—the Fathers of the Church confused Mary from Bethany with Mary Magdalene. In the allegorical reading of the passage, the two sisters are presented with two counterposed behaviors: Martha as the model of active and material life (the vanity of the world) and Mary as the model of contemplative and meditational life, meaning the spiritual dimension that is nourished by listening to the Word of Christ, therefore an example to be favored and followed. The separation and contraposition of the two ways of life was a subject discussed in the ambits of the Protestant Reformation. In Catholic tradition, Mary Magdalene became a model of monastic life, and a symbol of spiritual, contemplative love.

Rarely depicted standing (see *Christ in the House of Mary and Martha* by Palma il Vecchio, 1500), she is normally represented sitting at Jesus's feet in the humble posture of a disciple (see *Christ in the House of Martha and Mary* by Jan Vermeer, 1655).

To this interpretative thread we must add the theme of Mary Magdalene's conversion as encouraged by Martha, an episode that is not present in the gospels, but appears in sacred dramas, especially German ones, and in several literary traditions such as *Vitae Patrum* (1330) by Domenico Cavalca. Here, Martha speaks of Jesus to her sister who lives enveloped by sin and the pleasures of the flesh, a conversation that sparks in the Magdalene an initial call to religion. It is the theme of the novel *Maria Maddalena peccatrice e convertita* (1636) by Anton Giulio Brignole Sale. In this book, Martha convinces her sister, who is "accustomed to gazing with admiration at her own beauty in the mirror," to change her way of life because time is running out, and sooner or later her ephemeral beauty will wane. Mary Magdalene sees her reflection in the mirror, an emblem of vanity particularly present in the iconography that regards her: a metaphorical representation of the opposition between being and seeming to be.

A few rare works take up the unusual theme of the two sisters. See the mural *Conversione di Maddalena ad opera di Marta* (1370) in the church of Santa Maddalena in Rencio (13th century, South Tyrol); the engraving *Marta conduce Maddalena da Cristo* (around 1520) by Marcantonio Raimondi; and the painting *Martha and Mary Magdalene* (around 1598) by Caravaggio.

The theme of contemplation is not only linked to the episode between Martha and Mary, but is often blended with pictures of the penitent and the hermit, showing the Magdalene contemplating the Cross in the silence of the desert or in the solitude of her meditations.

Hermit. Confused with Mary of Egypt (as we saw), who is a redeemed prostitute leading a life of penitence in a cave, Mary Magdalene is represented in the guise of an anchoress, a model used as an invitation to ascesis and the refusal of worldly vanities.

> "In the meantime blessed Mary Magdalene, wishing to devote herself to heavenly contemplation, withdrew to a barren wilderness where she remained in anonymity for thirty years in a place prepared for her by the hands of angels."
>
> (Jacobus de Voragine *The Golden Legend* volume 4, *The Life of Saint Mary Magdalene*)

She generally is depicted in the clothing of a hermit, or covered only by her own hair. Beside her lies a skull, a source of meditation on death, and her body is marked by fasting. Sometimes she is alone; other times with John the Baptist or Saint Jerome (see the painter Jacopo da Sellaio, second half of the 15th century). The statue *Penitent Magdalene* by Donatello, sculpted for the Baptistery of Florence, is a typical example that indicates the consuming melancholy of ascetic life.

One variant on this theme is the Praying Magdalene, found in many paintings (see Antonio del Pollaiolo) and sculptures (see Andrea Cavalcanti).

It must be remarked how this iconography sometimes has the underlying theme of the portrayal of Eve—she too is represented as a beautiful, young nude woman, sensual and with long hair—to let emerge even more ambiguity and feminine charm.

Taken up to heaven. According to *The Golden Legend*, when Mary Magdalene lived a life of hermitage, every day she was carried up to heaven by angels.

"One day the Lord opened the eyes of this priest, and he saw quite clearly, with his own eyes, how the angels came down to the place where blessed Mary lived, lifted her in the air, and an hour later returned her to the same place, singing the praises of God." (Jacobus de Voragine *The Golden Legend* volume 4, *The Life of Saint Mary Magdalene*)

This is not an Assumption like the one regarding the Virgin Mary, when she is taken up to heaven after her death. Rather it is an elevation that occurred regularly at the hands of angels who—several times per day—lifted Mary Magdalene in the air so that she could listen to songs of glory, and then brought her back to earth. The image of Glory of Saint Mary Magdalene was especially used during the Counter-Reformation to present her to the faithful as an example of redemption from sin, seeing how, through remorse and penitence, she surpassed passions and attained heavenly glory. The colorful and sumptuous painting by Domenichino finds counterparts in ones by Giovanni Lanfranco and Morazzone, which are distinguished by an erotic accentuation of Mary Magdalene's nude body.

Linked to the same theme is *Mary Magdalene in Ecstasy*, which exalts the mystical transport given by God, testifying to her sanctity. Caravaggio's depiction shows her in ecstatic abandon, almost a languor of existence, similar to death. It influenced many artists, including Rubens, who exaggerates the ecstatic syncope; Simon Vouet, whose portrayal of her body is more markedly erotic for its unbridled femininity; and Guido Reni, whose ethereal Magdalene is dressed soberly, her gaze lifted to the sky.

As a subject of knowledge. Mary Magdalene represents the quest for knowledge.

> "Peter said to Mary: 'Sister, we know that the Savior loved you more than the rest of women. Tell us the words of the Savior which you remember—which you know (but) we do not, nor have we heard them.' Mary answered and said: 'What is hidden from you I will proclaim to you.'" (Gospel of Mary, 10:1-8)

In accordance with her being the protectress of the Dominicans, the painter Bartolomeo della Porta depicts her in the presence of God, being introduced to his mysteries while she is still alive. In his altarpiece *Eternal Father in Glory with the Saints Catherine of Siena and Mary Magdalene*, she wears a red dress and a light semi-transparent veil that covers her hair and cascades down her back. She is kneeling with a handkerchief in her right hand and a jar of ointment in her left hand.

In *The Disputation on the Trinity* (1517), Andrea del Sarto stages six saints animatedly discussing questions regarding the dogma of the Holy Trinity. Sebastian, Augustine of Hippo, Lawrence, Peter Martyr and Francis of Assisi are joined by a kneeling Mary Magdalene, the only woman present, clasping an urn of unguent in the bottom half of the picture.

A personal and conversational encounter in the name of love and knowledge, instead of a theological dispute, is the subject of *Cristo e la Maddalena* (1954) by Giorgio De Chirico, where the two subjects are portrayed in the foreground looking at each other in a mirrored image.

Apostoless and preacheress. One last theme, little explored in art history, but certainly the most significant for the current question of the role of women in the Church, is that of the Preaching Magdalene.

> "So Mary of Magdala went and told the disciples that she had seen the Lord and that he had said these things to her." (Gospel of John 20:18)

> "When the blessed Mary Magdalene saw the people streaming to the shrine to do sacrifice to the idols, she got up, quite calmly, and, with a serene expression on her face and with measured words, began to turn them from their idol worship, and with great single-mindedness to preach the Gospel of Christ."
> (*The Golden Legend* volume 4, *The Life of Saint Mary Magdalene*)

Sent by Christ to the disciples to announce his resurrection, Mary Magdalene is rarely represented in the role of the preacheress, which is why several mediaeval miniatures are extremely precious, such as one found in the Saint Albans Psalter (first half of the 12th century), an English illuminated manuscript commissioned by Christina of Markyate. Here we see Mary Magdalene announcing Jesus's resurrection to the apostles with great authority. Another is the miniature found in the Gospels of Henry the Lion, where the woman advances dynamically in front of seven listening apostles. Mary Magdalene is represented with her head covered and wearing a dress and mantle from former times. She is standing before Peter, who underlines her authority by pointing her out to the other apostles and bearing a sign that reads, "Tell us Mary, what you saw along the road" (*Dic nobis, Maria, quid vidisti in via*). The apostoless holds a banner with the answer: "The tomb of the living Christ and I saw the glory of his rising." (*Sepulcrum Christi viventis et gloriam vidi resurgentis.*)

Analogous representations of her bringing the announcement to the disciples are found at the Notre-Dame Cathedral of Chartres in the stained-glass window (1200-1205) that depicts scenes from the life of Mary Magdalene; in the Ingeborg Psalter (around 1200); and in the Queen Mary Psalter (around 1320).

The pictures of her as an announcer of the Gospel, however, are mostly connected to the legend that imagines her arriving by boat in Marseille intent on converting the pagan people to Christianity.

In the Florentine panel painting *Mary Magdalene with Eight Scenes from her Life* (mentioned in Chapters 3 and 6), we find the episode where Mary Magdalene preaches to women and men in a setting of city architecture (right-hand column, second picture from top), where all are listening intently.

Yet this iconographic theme did not find much popularity in modern or contemporary art. Only a few years ago has it been reprised in several depictions originating in the context of theology of feminist liberation and exegesis. While in reception history, "seeing the Lord" by the apostles and Paul has represented the basis for universal and lasting apostolate, the evangelizing function of Mary Magdalene was reduced to a short-term announcement service that was not incisive to the life of women in the Church. In this sense, art responds to the ecclesiastical and political sensibilities of the times.

Indubitably, after the Virgin Mary, the Magdalene is the best loved and most depicted female figure. She is a lover, friend, follower and faithful companion, a bringer of desire for redemption, knowledge, spiritual renewal, missionary commitment and more.

Many lines of interpretation intersect in her, generating varied artistic creations, multiple occasions for devotion and just as many opportunities for reflection on the female image.

CHAPTER 7
THE MAGDALENE BEYOND THE MAGDALENE

The research in this book is not merely an exercise in archeological philology, but aims to start a hermeneutic revolution, to the extent that it pertains to much broader fields beyond the historical figure of Mary Magdalene, and touches the very heart of Christianity. The case of Mary Magdalene is a window for reflection upon the importance of the role played by Jesus's female disciples, but not only that. The significant presence of the women in the communities of the origins is connected to several important theological nodes regarding the male monopoly of the doctrinal patrimony and the institutional bodies of some Churches that have contributed historically to the exclusion of women. For these reasons, interrogation is needed regarding our comprehension of the Bible and its erroneous interpretations; regarding the weight of tradition in the elaboration of the anthropological vision; regarding the sexual taboo linked to the dynamics of gender; regarding the exclusion of women from the apostolic succession and from decision-making roles in the Church; regarding the identity of the community of faith in the light of the evangelic message and the recent advancements having to do with the dignity and equality of the human person, male and female.

Women and Bible: false interpretations

In 1838, the Quaker Sarah Grimké answered the congregational ministers of Massachusetts with particular determination. Referring to the request made by the apostle Paul to the Christian women of Corinth "to remain quiet at meetings since they have no permission to speak" (I Corinthians 14:34), these ministers strongly objected to women speaking in public. Grimké placed the biblical question at the center of the battle for women's emancipation: "The New Testament has been referred to, and I am willing to abide by its decisions, but must enter my protest against the false translation of some passages by the MEN who did that work, and against the perverted interpretation by the MEN who undertook to write commentaries thereon." (Sarah Grimké, *Letters on the Equality of the Sexes, and the Condition of Woman*, 1838)

In the same years, the Afro-American Methodist preacher Jarena Lee was demonstrating how the different reading of the holy scripture by women would allow them a more active participation in the life of Churches. It was precisely the experience of Mary Magdalene that offered the theological arguments to affirm women's rights.

"For as unseemly as it may appear now-a-days for a woman to preach, it should be remembered that nothing is impossible with God. And why should it be thought impossible, heterodox, or improper for a woman to preach, seeing the Saviour died for the woman as well as for the man? If the man may preach, because the Saviour died for him, why not the woman, seeing he died for her also? [. . .] Did not Mary *first* preach the risen Saviour, and is not the doctrine of the resurrection the very climax of Christianity? Hangs not all our hope on this, as argued by Saint Paul? Then did not Mary, a woman, preach the gospel? For she preached the resurrection of the crucified Son of God."

(Jarena Lee, *Religious Experience and Journal of Mrs. Jarena Lee, giving an account of her call to preach the gospel*, 1849)

The Bible Bands, a female network of bible study groups founded in 1884 in Protestant Afro-American communities in the United States, represented a pioneering attempt to reappropriate the holy scripture in order to attest to authoritative and prophetic roles practiced by women, of which the Bible preserves the memory. The Bible Bands contested the stereotype of women's passivity and fragility. Their experiences led to the necessity of rereading the Scriptures to discern contradictions and unmask the manipulation that legitimized the discrimination of women. The efforts converged in *The Woman's Bible* (1895) by the American suffragist Elizabeth Cady Stanton. This truly political act was meant to free women from the situation of subordination determined by patriarchal contexts in which the holy texts were elaborated, and above all, free them from a false and consolidated exegesis that penalized the female gender.

In the 150 years since the birth of biblical feminism, Mary Magdalene has been considered an emblematic figure.

The correct narration of her story casts light on the complex relationship between the Scriptures and women, in two ways. One encourages a more trustworthy reconstruction of the biblical characters presented in cultural contexts marked by patriarchy; and the other shows the repercussions that these interpretations have had and still have on our social and ecclesiastical structure. It is undeniable that in the history of the exegesis of the New Testament, several female figures have been distorted and tamed, resulting in models of silence (Mary of Bethany), caregiving (Martha), penitence (Mary Magdalene), contemplation (the Samaritan woman) and obedience (Mary of Nazareth) instead of examples of active, authoritative discipleship, which has influenced in a decisive manner the separation of functions and tasks between the sexes.

The question of how women are presented within the holy text, and the question of recognition for the role they effectively practiced are much more complex matters. Their diminishment is present in the communities of the origins, and the gospels do not hide the disciples' embarrassment and sometimes disagreement with the relationship of dialogue and equality established by Jesus with the female universe.

Current exegetic studies show how the canonical texts are the product of a series of cultural dynamics and conflicts between groups in which the relationships between the sexes had their weight. The work of critical decoding that has been furthered in recent years by female exegetes has freed the biblical women from silence, misinterpretation and sometimes even mystification by recognizing the primary role they had in constituting Christianity. At the same time, it has reopened ancient questions surrounding the correctness of interpretative methods, the formation of the canon, and the relation between Scriptures and tradition.

Tradition: misunderstanding and manipulation

Just as in biblical exegesis we must speak of a range of possible interpretative solutions instead of a univocal scheme, also tradition, being subject to the dynamics of history, knows a variety of currents that contradict the doctrinal transmission presented as the only one possible. We must not neglect the existence of texts in the margins of the official doctrine (Apocrypha, Gnostics and heretic writings) in addition to those considered canonical. Also these are the fruit of theological choices and political compromises. All are part of a plurality of positions that has much to say about the varied and complex phenomenon linked to the birth of the Christian religion.

Mary Magdalene is the touchstone of the polyvalence of these texts, which variously underline the centrality of her person in the constitution of the community of faith (John), show her opposed to the leadership of Peter (the Gnostic gospels), or contrariwise downsize her in comparison with the apostles (Luke), or even remove her by not acknowledging her presence, to the extent of making her invisible (Paul).

Evidently, the recognition of female guidance and what

role to entrust to women were subjects of intense debate within the communities of the first centuries—we have significant traces of this in the first Christian literature. In different groups from Asia Minor, there was a presence of Christian women who, in reference to biblical figures and often to Mary Magdalene, exercised prophetic, pastoral and ministerial functions.

But those groups were placed in the margins and the richness of experiences was drastically reduced and channeled into garbled and stereotyped images. The figure of Mary Magdalene prevalently presented as the repentant prostitute concealed all apostolic dimensions. Fictitious narrations produced misunderstandings and prejudices that have been difficult to overcome in the religious imagery of Christians.

Knowing the richness of our historical patrimony, which today we understand better in its varied expressions, can help us overcome misperceptions and manipulations. This makes it necessary to consider "tradition" as "an entire range of traditions"– that is, as a differentiated, complicated cultural transmission involving multiple and numerous subjects, groups and movements.

In the case of Mary Magdalene, we are in the presence of women and men who in different eras of history, in her memory, have given life to experiences of faith, acts of worship, artwork, institutions, doctrinal elaborations, spiritual texts, ecclesiastical proposals and more. All this cannot be uncritically enclosed in a univocal proposition.

Sexual taboo

Starting with the false identification of Mary Magdalene as the repentant prostitute, her figure favored the demonization of female sexuality and sensuality, which in order to be redeemed needed penitence and mortification. The "beautiful woman" became a catalyst for the erotic imagination of men, who imbued her body with desire, frustration and a sense of guilt.

It is undeniable that Mary Magdalene interpreted as a prostitute speaks through her physique, and her interactions with Jesus are marked by a powerful carnal dimension. While her body has known sexual relations with other men, she nevertheless establishes with the Teacher from Nazareth a physical vicinity that is conceded to no other woman, and that has been well represented by art history. It is physical contact made of gestures such as kissing his feet, touching his hair, wanting to anoint his corpse and wanting to hold him back once she has recognized him as risen. The encounter with Jesus on Easter morning in the garden evokes the love-struck maiden's search for her beloved in the *Song of Songs* (Chapter 3), a love canticle par excellence, its narration full of sensual eroticism. In the Gospel of John, the love of Mary Magdalene weeping over the empty tomb and the absence of Jesus's body is a prelude to reciprocal recognition ("Mary!" "Rabbuni!", John 20:16) and the apostolic investiture vis à vis the disciples. But in traditional patristics, attention is focused on the physical contact the woman would like to have with Christ by touching him and detaining him. Attention is also given to the fact that he then distances himself from her because he lives in a new existential dimension ("Do not cling to me," John 20:17). In patristic tradition, comments on this passage are influenced by the preconception of seeing womanhood as a source of enticement from which a man must steer clear.

The representation of Mary Magdalene is hereby conditioned by a negative view of sexuality that soon entered Christian thought, marked since the first centuries by the insertion of Encratite tendencies (rigorous self-control), and by the recovery of the view that a woman's body is impure (Leviticus 15:19-30), despite Jesus's acts to the contrary. While functional to procreation, sexual activity was still considered a road to sin, and pleasure was its fruit. Containment of passions, discipline over desire, and control of sexual impulse were considered crucial in order to live a worthy life of faith marked by virginity and matrimonial continence.

Subjected to severe discipline, sexuality was an obsession of Christian society, which went on to radicalize ascetic values, especially with the diffusion and success of the monastic formula, and brought with it the imposition of sexual abstinence even for married clergy. For single men, purity became a symbol of superiority and priestly sacredness that should not be contaminated by contact with the impurity of the female gender. The *Noli me tangere* episode somehow emphasized Jesus's detachment from all physical contact with women, strengthening the sexual taboo with regard to his person, too. The distance he took from the female body became a model and a warning for the celibate clergy. Unsurprisingly, art privileged the *Noli me tangere* sentence from John the evangelist to the total detriment of the apostolic mission that completed the theological meaning of that same passage: "But go and find the brothers, and tell them," says the Risen One to Mary Magdalene in John 20:17.

Apostolic succession and power in the Church

"Peter is not under the cross, while Mary is. Neither Peter nor any of the Twelve attend the burial of the Teacher or is at the tomb on Easter morning. Instead, Mary and the other female disciples are there." *Mary of Magdala: Revisiting the Sources* by Marinella Perroni and Cristina Simonelli, 2016 (English translation from 2019).

Mary Magdalene is at the origins of the community of faith because she is the witness of the resurrection. She creates the transition from the historical Jesus to the Christ of faith; she has the decisive word: "So Mary of Magdala went and told the disciples that she had seen the Lord and that he had said these things to her." (John 20:18)

Although she receives the apostolic investiture from Christ who sends her to the apostles, the assignment soon disappeared. On the list of apparitions that Paul receives from a former tradition and that he writes down and legitimizes (I Corinthians 15), the Magdalene's name has vanished to the full advantage of a male-only chain of witnesses who range from Peter to "more than 500 brothers" (*Mary of Magdala: Revisiting the Sources*).

Therefore, her investiture must have created many difficulties by entering into competition with Peter's (see the Gnostic gospels). As a consequence, the definition of the canon, the establishment of the criteria of orthodoxy, and the institutional order of the ancient Church expelled Mary Magdalene from the apostolic succession, recognizing it only to men, seeing that only males could legitimately be assigned to posts of authority.

The Episcopalian institution and the rigorously male hierarchical organization of the religious community became the sole and absolute model. The network of apostolic succession was considered a warrant of the custody and transmission of the message of Christ (Irenaeus, *Against Heresies* Book 3, 1). Its legitimacy was based on the improper identification of the Twelve (interpreted not with the symbolic meaning of ecclesia as the new Israel, but as twelve men that Jesus called his disciples) as well as the apostles (the term apostle in the writings of the New Testament was not reserved only for men). The requisites required of apostles correspond to the experiences of the women, too: being eyewitnesses of the resurrection; having received the mandate of preaching from the Lord (I Corinthians 9:1); and having been disciples on Jesus's earthly travels (Acts 1:21-22).

Today's recognition and rehabilitation of Mary Magdalene as an apostle; today's inclusive model of participation; and today's ethics of equality reopen for discussion the following issues: the terms of the female exercise of authority; the question of the governance of the Church (ecclesiastical polity) and of women's representation within it. For centuries, erasing her role as an apostle has barred women from ministerial roles. Her rediscovery can only favor a profound rethinking of the institution and its ecclesiastic identity.

Mary Magdalene's exegetic story is a further step toward the deconstruction of the ancient Church's organizational models, which stand in need of critical analysis in all their elements to become the subject of modifications and adaptions. Institutional aspects, too, respond to historical change. The set of rules that the Church has given itself cannot be considered an irrevocable and definite identity.

The case of Mary Magdalene must be inserted in the broader analysis of the presence of women in the history of Christianity in view of a reconstruction of relationship models that are more appropriate for an inclusive Church that is in accordance with the liberating practice of Jesus. This is why it is necessary to rework the traditional ecclesiological models according to the principle of baptismal and apostolic "joint responsibility," which is more suited to today's sensibility in its attentiveness to women's dignity and representation. Women can no longer be excluded from the major organs of Church government.

As the prototype of apostolic faith, Mary Magdalene through her words and testimony allows the group of disciples to find a salvific meaning in the death of the man Jesus. The foundational character of her experience tells us that neither she nor any woman should be belittled, for they are full-fledged subjects of the community of faith, including all that concerns the functions of ministry and leadership. In imitation of the practice of the Teacher, the community should not have repeated the male hierarchic structure that existed in the unequal society of the time. Rather it should have created conviviality based on diaconal functions and the equal assumption of responsibility. In addition, the connotative identity of being male or female disciples, called upon to construct a fellowship, did not make a distinction between the sexes. Women freed from their exclusion must be inserted in this reference frame.

The figure of Mary Magdalene as a disciple and an apostle is emblematic, a stimulating indication of a path that can bring clarity within the ecclesiastic community founded on tending to others. "This is not to happen among you. No, anyone who wants to become great among you must be your servant, and anyone who wants to be first among you must be slave to all." (Mark 10:43-44)

FURTHER READING
(MOSTLY IN ITALIAN)

I have limited myself to suggesting a certain number of studies. For a more complete bibliography, readers can refer to the collection of essays edited by Edmondo Lupieri, *Una sposa per Gesù. Maria Maddalena tra antichità e postmoderno* (Carocci, Rome 2017). What follows is a list of the most recent and significant studies, organized by theme.

The main results of the excavations of Magdala Project related to the hypothesis of there having existed a town named Magdala on Lake Tiberias and identifying it, have resulted in many contributions published by the participating archaeologists. Such papers include *Scoperte archeologiche recenti attorno al Lago di Galilea: contributo allo studio dell'ambiente del Nuovo Testamento e del Gesù storico* by Stefano De Luca published in *Terra Sancta: archeologia ed esegesi* edited by Giorgio Paximadi and Marcello Fidanzio (Eupress FTL, Lugano 2013, pages 18–111); *Magdala As We Now Know It* by Richard Bauckham and Stefano De Luca published in *Early Christianity* issue 6, 2015, pages 91–118; and *Magdala of Galilee: A Jewish City in the Hellenistic and Roman Period* by Richard Bauckham (Baylor University, Waco, Texas 2018). The study by Joan

E. Taylor titled *Missing Magdala and the Name of Mary "Magdalene"* published in *Palestine Exploration Quarterly* issue 3, 2014, pages 205–223 is critical of several interpretations related to localizing the town of Magdala and the name attributed to the discipless of Jesus. Taylor's paper take up a thesis advanced by Maria Luisa Rigato titled *Ancora riflessioni su colei che fu chiamata la Resa grande* published in *Studia Patavina* issue 50, 2003, pages 727–752.

There have been many exegetic studies that give clarity to the evangelic figure of Mary Magdalene, starting with *Jésus a-t-il-été oint plusieurs fois et par plusieurs femmes?* by Réginald Garrigou-Lagrange published in *Revue biblique* issue 9, 1912, pages 504–532. More recent ones I'd like to mention are: *Maria di Magdala, santa calunniata e glorificata* by Gianfranco Ravasi published in *Maddalena* by Giovanni Testori with an introduction and notes by G. Ravasi (Franco Maria Ricci, Milan 1989, pages 15–24); *Maria di Magdala e le molte altre* by Carla Ricci (D'Auria, Naples 1991); *Tra/sfigurazione. Il personaggio evangelico di Maria di Magdala e il mito della peccatrice redenta nella tradizione occidentale* by Lilia Sebastiani (Queriniana, Brescia 1992); *Maria di Magdala, prima apostola?* by Andrea Taschl-Erber published in *I Vangeli. Narrazioni e storia* by Mercedes Navarro Puerto and Marinella Perroni in the series "La Bibbia e le donne", 2.1 published by Il Pozzo di Giacobbe, Trapani 2012, pages 375–397; and *Maria di Magdala. Una genealogia apostolica* by Marinella Perroni and Cristina Simonelli published by Aracne editrice, Ariccia 2016.

For a wider look at Jesus's female following, I recommend Raymond E. Brown's classic book on the roles of women in the Johannine communities, *The Community of the Beloved Disciple: The Life, Loves, and Hates of an Individual Church in New Testament Times* (1979), and a fundamental text for feminist exegetics, *In Memory of Her: A Feminist Theological Reconstruction of Christian Origins* (1983) by Elisabeth Schüssler Fiorenza. Since then, studies on the women in the gospels have multiplied all over the world. Recent Italian ones include *Volti di donna nel Quarto Vangelo* by Arianna Rotondo published in *Annali di Studi Religiosi* issue 6, 2005, pages 287–305; *Discepole di Gesù* by Marinella Perroni published in *Donne e Bibbia. Storia ed esegesi* edited by Adriana Valerio (EDB, Bologna 2006); *Il profumo del vangelo. Gesù incontra le donne* by Nuria Calduch-Benages (Paoline, Milan 2007); *Svolte. Donne negli snodi del cammino di Gesù* by Lilia Sebastiani (Cittadella, Assisi 2008); *Discepole di Gesù* by Maria Luisa Rigato (EDB, Bologna 2011); *Discepole, ma non apostole: l'opera di Luca* by Marinella Perroni published in *I Vangeli. Narrazioni e storia* (opus citatum, pages 177–214); and *Dentro e fuori le "case". Trasformazione dei ruoli femminili dal movimento di Gesù alle chiese protocristiane* by Adriana Destro and Mauro Pesce published in *I Vangeli. Narrazioni e storia* (opus citatum, pages 293–311).

On the mistaken identity that confuses Mary Magdalene with Mary of Bethany: *Marta di Betania. Dai testi alle immagini* by Chiara Macor (Effatà, Cantalupa 2019). On the meaning of the anointment, erroneously attributed to Mary Magdalene: *Maria di Betania e l'unzione di Gesù* by Renzo Infante published in *Vetera Christianorum* issue 37, 2000, pages 35–55; and *Uomini e donne nella prassi discepolare: diaconia e potere nell'unzione di Betania (Gv 12, 1–8)* by Arianna Rotondo published in *Annali di Storia dell'Esegesi* issue 2, 2017, pages 553–575. On a number of evocative and provocative interpretations such as the origins of her name, and the hypothesis that Mary Magdalene was the favorite disciple or the author of the fourth gospel: *Mary Magdalene: Author of the Fourth Gospel?* by Ramon K. Jusino (http://ramon_k_jusino.tripod.com/magdalene.html), 1998; *The Fourth Gospel: Tales of a Jewish Mystic* (2013) by John Shelby Spong; and *Nel nome di Maria* by Antonella Salvati published by Atheneum, Florence 2013.

The author recommends the following apocryphal literature: *Gli apocrifi del Nuovo Testamento* edited by Mario Erbetta and published by Marietti, Casale Monferrato 1975 and *Apocrifi del Nuovo Testamento* edited by Luigi Moraldi and published by Utet, Milan 1971. A general study is found in *I vangeli apocrifi* by Claudio Gianotto published by Il Mulino, Bologna 2009. More specifically for Mary Magdalene, there are the following: *"Zerstört die Werke der Weiblichkeit!" Maria Magdalena, Salome und andere Jüngerinnen Jesu in christlich-gnostischen Schriften* by Silke Petersen published by Brill, Leiden 1999; *The Gospel of Mary of Magdala: Jesus and the First Woman Apostle* by Karen L. King published by Polebridge Press, Santa Rosa, California 2003; *Un'apostola tra spiritualità e conflitto. Tradizioni apocrife* by Cristina Simonelli published in *Maria di Magdala* (opus citatum) by Perroni and

Simonelli, pages 125–184; *Maria Maddalena. L'amata di Gesù nei testi apocrifi* by Carla Ricci published by Claudiana, Turin 2017; *Discepola prediletta e annunciatrice di rivelazione: La Maddalena nella letteratura gnostica* by Cambry Pardee published in *Una sposa per Gesù* (opus citatum) by Lupieri, pages 59–84.

Regarding the multiple natures of Mary Magdalene under the Fathers of the Church: *La Maddalena e il Risorto: esegesi patristica di Gv 20 (1–2. 11–18)* by Marcello Marin in *L'Apostola. Maria Maddalena inascoltata verità* edited by Carla Ricci and Marcello Marin published by Palomar, Bari 2006 pages 49–80; *La santa dalle molteplici identità: viaggio intorno a Maria di Magdala* by Elena Giannarelli published in *Il riposo nella Tenda* issue 34, 2009, pages 9–31; *La Maddalena patristica* by Amanda Kunder published in *Una sposa per Gesù* (opus citatum) by Lupieri, pages 109–126. Regarding the Byzantine world: *Sainte Marie-Madeleine dans la tradition orthodoxe* by Lucretia Vasilescu published in *L'Apostola* (opus citatum) pages 297–325.

About the development of her cult in the Middle Ages: *Le culte de Marie-Madeleine en Occident, des origines à la fin du moyen âge* by Victor Saxer published by Clavreuil, Auxerre-Paris 1959; the *Maria Maddalena* entry compiled by Victor Saxer in *Bibliotheca Sanctorum*, VIII, Rome 1967, columns 1078–1104; *Mary of Magdala: The Evolution of her Role in Medieval Drama* by John R. Kane published in *Studi Medievali* issue 26, 1985 pages 677–684; *The Making of the Magdalen: Preaching and Popular Devotion in the Later Middle Ages* by Katherine Ludwig Jansen published by Princeton University Press, Princeton 1999; *Maria*

*Maddalena tra oriente e occidente: Romano il Melode e
Gregorio Magno* by Renzo Infante published in *Studia
Antiqua et Archaeologica* issue 12, 2006, pages 135–150;
and *Apostola e peccatrice: ricezione medievale di Maria di
Magdala* by Andrea Taschl-Erber published in *Donne e
Bibbia nel Medioevo (secoli XII-XV)* edited by Kari
Børresen and Adriana Valerio (La Bibbia e le Donne, 7.2),
Il Pozzo di Giacobbe, Trapani 2011, pages 295–318.

On the history of Magdalene institutions: *Maddalene* by
A. Martinez Cuesta in *Dizionario degli Istituti di Perfezione*
published by Paoline, Rome 1978, columns 801–812.

For literary interpretations in the modern age: *Il tema
letterario della Maddalena nell'età della Controriforma* by
Salvatore Ussia in *Rivista di Storia e Letteratura religiosa*
issue 3, 1988, pages 385–424; *Donne e Chiesa. Una storia di
genere* by Adriana Valerio published by Carocci, Rome
2016; *Per "sfiammeggiar di un vivo e ardente amore."
Vittoria Colonna, Bernardino Ochina e la Maddalena* by
Michele Camaioni in *El Orbe Católico* edited by Maria
Lupi and Claudio Rolle, Ril, Santiago de Chile 2016, pages
105-106; *Maria Maddalena peccatrice santa tra narrazione e
scena. Un percorso cinque-seicentesco* by Quinto Marini in
Sacro e/o profano nel teatro fra Rinascimento ed età dei lumi
edited by Stella Castellaneta and Francesco Saverio
Minervini, published by Cacucci, Bari 2009, pages 97–128;
*"Lasciva e penitente". Nuovi sondaggi sul tema della
Maddalena nella poesia religiosa del Seicento* by Luca Piantoni
in *Studi Secenteschi* issue 54, 2013, pages 25–48; *L'ombra di
Maddalena* by Anna Maria Pedullà in *L'Italianistica oggi:
ricerca e didattica* edited by Beatrice Alfonzetti, Teresa

Cancro, Valeria Di Iasio and Ester Pietrobon, published by Adi editore, Rome 2017, pages 1–11.

For iconographic studies, I refer to the entry *Madeleine* complied by Louis Réau in *Iconographie de l'art chrétien*, volume 3 published by Presses Universitaires de France, Paris 1958, pages 846–859; to the fascinating and eloquent text *Maddalena* by Testori, (opus citatum) with its wealth of literary and artistic references, and to two exhibitions: one in Florence under the curatorship of Marilena Mosco, "La Maddalena tra sacro e profano, da Giotto a De Chirico" (catalogue by Mondadori, Milan 1986) and the other one in Loreto curated by Vittorio Sgarbi, "La Maddalena tra peccato e penitenza" 2016. More specifically on medieval art, there is *Maria Maddalena. Storia e iconografia nel Medioevo dal III al XIV secolo* by Viviana Vannucci published by Gangemi, Rome 2012. Regarding Caravaggio: *L'iconografia della Maria Maddalena a Napoli* by Vincenzo Pacelli published by Electa, Naples 2006. Regarding the modern age: *L'iconografia di Maria Maddalena nel Novecento* by Fiorella Nicosia published in *L'Apostola* (opus citatum) pages 153–184.

For the questions of theological and ecclesiastical nature that the figure of Mary Magdalene raises, and for the consequences they have on the role of women in the Church, I refer to two of my studies, *Donne e Chiesa. Una storia di genere* published by Carocci, Rome 2016 and *Il potere delle donne nella Chiesa* published by Laterza, Rome–Bari 2016, both by Adriana Valerio.

Notes

1. INTRODUCTION: ...

Hennig, ... Conflict ... ... (Oxford: ... ...
Macmillan, ... Quoted in Buchanan, Michael Mann: On the
Queen. Arrogance & arrogance of Larry Mortimer theater of ... ...
(Publication, Kevin, ...

2. CHAPTER: 'What Is ...' THE JACOBEAN

A work on English ... ... from the Old ... New
Testament ... ... in Jonathan ...

Leslie ... ... Mary Magdalene, ... in
... ...

https://www.history.com/topic/...

Richard ... ...
... ...

Report ... ...
... ...

Martin ... ...
Peter Coverdale, ... by ...
Roberts and Jane, ... Christian ... Publishing, New
York, NY ... ...

3. CHAPTER: THE ... ...

Carlton ... ...
... ... edited by ... ... J. Pettit, and James Robinson (New ...,
... ...

Page Reed, ... Schmitt (Mill Valley: New
... ... James Joyce, 1, ...

NOTES

INTRODUCTION

[1] Honorius of Autun, *Speculum Ecclesiae: De Sancta Maria Magdalena*, PL 172, col 979. Quoted in Benedicta Ward, *Harlots of the Desert: A Study of Repentance in Early Monastic Studies* (Cistercian Publications, Kalamazoo, MI 1987), p. 16.

CHAPTER 1. WHO WAS THE MAGDALENE?

[2] For this English-language edition, all quotes from the Old and New Testaments were taken from the Jerusalem Bible.

[3] *Wikipedia, The Free Encyclopedia*, s.v. "Mary Magdalene," Note b (accessed April 13, 2021),
https://en.wikipedia.org/wiki/Mary_Magdalene.

[4] *Patristic Bible Commentary*: *St. Ambrose of Milan Commentary on Luke*, 24:1-12 (accessed April 13, 2021),
https://sites.google.com/site/aquinasstudybible/home/luke-commentary/ambrose-on-luke-24.

[5] *Ante-Nicene Fathers. Volume 4: Tertullian, Part Fourth; Minucius Felix; Commodian; Origen, Part First and Second*, edited by Alexander Roberts and James Donaldson (Christian Literature Publishing, New York, NY 1885).

CHAPTER 2. THE "COMPANION" OF JESUS IN GNOSTIC LITERATURE

[6] Citations from the Gnostic gospels were taken from *Nag Hammadi Studies*, edited by Martin Krause and James Robinson (Brill, Leiden 1979).

[7] *Pistis Sophia*, edited by Carl Schmidt (Brill, Leiden 1978).

[8] Quoted in Antti Marjanen, *The Woman Jesus Loved: Mary*

Magdalene in the Nag Hammadi Library and Related Documents (Brill, Leiden 1996), p. 206.

[9] Quoted in Margaret Alexiou, *After Antiquity: Greek Language, Myth, and Metaphor* (Cornell University Press, Ithaca, NY 2002), p. 449.

[10] *The New Testament Apocrypha*, edited by M. R. James (Clarendon Press, Oxford 1924).

[11] *Woodbrooke Studies: Christian Documents in Syriac, Arabic, and Garshuni*, edited and translated with a critical apparatus by Alphonse Mingana (W. Heffer & Sons, Cambridge 1928).

[12] *Book of the Resurrection, Gospel of Saint Bartholomew* in James (ed.), *The Apocryphal New Testament*, cit.

CHAPTER 3. PLURAL MIDDLE AGES

[13] Quoted in Alexiou, *After Antiquity*, cit., p. 437.

[14] *Patristic Bible Commentary*: *Gregory the Great Homily 25 on the Gospels*, accessed April 13, 2021),
https://sites.google.com/site/aquinasstudybible/home/gospel-of-john-commentary/gregory-the-great-homily-25-on-the-gospels.

[15] *Patristic Bible Commentary*: *Gregory the Great Homily 33 on the Gospels* (accessed April 13, 2021),
https://sites.google.com/site/aquinasstudybible/home/luke-commentary/gregory-the-great-homily-33-on-the-gospels.

[16] Quoted in Scott Wells, *Negotiating Community and Difference in Medieval Europe* (Brill, Leiden 2009), p. 156.

[17] Quoted in Deirdre Good, *Mariam, the Magdalen, and the Mother* (Indiana University Press, Bloomington, IN 2005), p. 20.

[18] Jacobus de Voragine, *The Golden Legend*, translated by Christopher Stace (Penguin Classics, London 1988).

CHAPTER 4. INTERPRETATIONS AND DOUBTS IN THE MODERN AGE

[19] Desiderius Erasmus, *Collected Works: Colloquies*, edited and translated by Craig Ringwalt Thompson (University of Toronto Press, Toronto 1997), pp. 504-5.

[20] *Disputatio Nova Contra Mulieres/A New Argument Against Women: a critical translation from the Latin with commentary, together with the original Latin text of 1595*, edited by Clive Hart (Edwin Mellen Press, Lewiston, NY 1998), p. 67.

CHAPTER 5. THE MAGDALENE OUTSIDE AND INSIDE THE PRESENT TIME

[21] Johann Wolfgang von Goethe, *Faust: Parts I & II*, translated by A. S. Kline (Poetry in Translation, 2003).

[22] Ernest Renan, *The Life of Jesus*, translated by Charles Edwin Wilbour (Carleton, New York, NY 1864).

[23] Marguerite Yourcenar, *Fires*, translated by Dori Katz (Farrar, Straus & Giroux, New York, NY 1981).

[24] José Saramago, *The Gospel According to Jesus Christ*, translated by Giovanni Pontiero (Houghton Mifflin Harcourt, New York, NY 1994).

[25] Dan Brown, *The Da Vinci Code* (Anchor Books, New York, NY 2003).

CHAPTER 6. ICONOGRAPHIC IMAGES AND SYMBOLS

[26] Jean-Luc Nancy, *Noli Me Tangere*, translated by Sarah Clift, Pascale-Anne Brault, and Michael Naas (Fordham University Press, New York, NY 2008), p. 23.

About the Author

Adriana Valerio is a historian and theologian. For over thirty years, since she became one of the first women in Italy to obtain a theology degree, she has devoted herself to the critical interpretation of the role of women within the history of Christianity. She is the author of many essays on the subject and an internationally recognized scholar.